Creating Projects to Ignite Learning
for Every Student

PROJECT BASED LEARNING

HANDBOOK

FOR MIDDLE & HIGH SCHOOL

BUCK INSTITUTE FOR EDUCATION

About PBLWorks–Buck Institute for Education

PBLWorks is the world's leading provider of high-quality resources and professional development for Project Based Learning. Its vision is that all students, no matter where they live or what their background, should have access to quality PBL instruction to deepen their learning and achieve success in college, career, and life. Its parent organization, the Buck Institute for Education, is a mission-driven not-for-profit 501(c)3 organization based in Novato, California, and is beneficiary of the Leonard and Beryl Buck Trust. Across the United States and around the world, PBLWorks provides PBL professional development to teachers and school leaders, as well as long-term support to partner schools and districts. PBLWorks also hosts the annual PBL World conference and offers online resources and courses at www.pblworks.org.

PROJECT BASED LEARNING HANDBOOK FOR MIDDLE AND HIGH SCHOOL

Authors: John Larmer, Eric White, Erin Brandvold, Feroze Munshi, Heather Wolpert-Gawron, Honor Moorman, James Fester, Laureen Adams, Sarah Field

Editor: John Larmer

Copyright © 2021 PBLWorks

Published by PBLWorks
3 Hamilton Landing, Suite 220,
Novato, California 94949 USA
pblworks.org

April 2021: First Edition.

Printed by Unicorn Group, Novato, California.
Designed by Jean Orlebeke.

ISBN 978-0-9974222-5-2

TABLE OF CONTENTS

Acknowledgments

We would first like to acknowledge the thousands of teachers across the United States and around the world who enrich their students' lives with Project Based Learning. We are grateful for your ideas, inspiration, and determination. We also appreciate the school leaders who create the conditions for teachers that make PBL possible and effective for students, especially for those furthest from educational opportunity.

The PBLWorks National Faculty is a stellar group of PBL teachers, leaders, instructional coaches and consultants, and we thank them—present and emeritus members—for their incredibly valuable work. Many of them wrote blog posts and created projects, materials for teachers, and professional development services for PBLWorks from which we derived material for this book. Several members of the "NF" were co-authors of this book, and you can see their names on the back of the title page. This was truly a team effort!

Staff members at PBLWorks/Buck Institute for Education deserve credit for helping make these books happen and ensuring their quality. John Larmer set the direction for the books, led the writing team, and edited them. Lillian Dignan patiently managed the design and production process in the final months. Debbie Woo consulted on the concept, title and design. Debra Hunter provided expert feedback and guidance from the beginning. We are also grateful to staff members who read drafts and gave us kind, specific, and helpful feedback, particularly Sarah Field, Lisa Mireles, and Charity Parsons.

Sarah Field deserves special recognition for her always-available support and for leading the creation of the high-quality PBLWorks project library, from which we borrowed. Gina Olabuenaga created and contributed to many of PBLWorks's top-notch materials and professional development for teachers and school leaders, from which we drew. Laureen Adams and Dinah Becton-Consuegra helped shape our thinking about educational equity. Thank you, thank you.

To all students, and their futures.

✳ NOTES ✳

An Overview of PBL

WHY HAS PROJECT BASED LEARNING BECOME an increasingly popular and important feature of 21st century education, across the United States and around the world? Because Project Based Learning works, and it makes learning more meaningful for students.

What do we mean by "works" and "more meaningful"?

If you ask a teacher who's been implementing PBL successfully, they'll say it improves student learning. It promotes deeper learning, not just the acquisition of factual knowledge, and builds 21st century success skills. An engaging project motivates students to learn. A project in which young people tackle a real-world problem, challenge, or issue builds a sense of agency that can transform lives. A PBL teacher will also note that it makes their job more rewarding.

If you ask a student who's experienced high-quality PBL, they'll say something similar about why it works, in their own words. "I love PBL because it's like a secret. There's so much learning but you don't realize it. The teachers help us but students do most of the thinking. Sometimes, we think so much that our heads hurt," a 4th grader commented after a project. "Projects took the concepts we learned and made us apply them, challenging us to think critically and creatively," said a 12th grader. "It really, actually changed my life," said another high schooler about a project.

If you ask the family of a student who's experienced high-quality PBL, they will report that their learner is more engaged. "My son's reading skills went way up because he was motivated by projects," said a parent of a second grader. "We have been blown away by the passion, creativity, depth, and commitment she has shown," said a parent of a high school student. And caregivers note that when they ask the question, "What did you do in school today?" the answer isn't the typical "nothin"—instead it's enthusiastic news about the latest project.

If you ask a school leader who has helped build a PBL program and created the conditions for teachers do it well, they'll echo what teachers say. They'll be pleased with how pleased their students and families are. They might even say PBL has transformed their school's culture. If their school has created a "graduate profile" with a vision of students as critical thinkers, problem solvers, effective collaborators, responsible citizens, and project managers, they know PBL is a big part of how they will reach that vision. And they won't be worried about test scores (see more on this in the section to follow, "All Students Can Do PBL").

If you ask a researcher who's looked at high-quality PBL, they'll point to several studies showing its effectiveness—with the usual caveats, being researchers, about the nuances involved and the need for more studies. PBL has been shown to have positive effects on student learning outcomes, including those measured by standardized tests, as well as problem-solving and other success skills, plus engagement, motivation, and self-efficacy. (See the section to follow, "PBL's Effectiveness" on the evidence from research.)

What Is Project Based Learning?

First, let's define Project Based Learning formally as:

> *A teaching method in which students gain knowledge and skills by working for an extended period of time to investigate and respond to an authentic, engaging, and complex question, problem, or challenge, and make their work public.*

We like to say that in PBL, learning comes alive for students, and it unleashes a creative, contagious energy in the classroom (or wherever students are learning).

Project Based Learning is a form of "active learning" in which students often work in collaboration with others. It falls into the general category of inquiry-based learning. Other inquiry-based approaches include research papers, scientific investigations, and Socratic discussions. Problem-based learning, also known as PBL, is a close cousin to our model and shares most of the same characteristics.

The methodology of Project Based Learning is derived from progressive education and constructivist learning theories, which emphasize the role of the learner in constructing knowledge through experience, reflection, and incorporation of new information into pre-existing knowledge—rather than just passively absorbing information. Contemporary models of PBL draw from the work of Jean Piaget, Lev Vygotsky, Paolo Freire, and especially John Dewey.

Dewey, who we consider the grandfather of PBL, advocated "learning by experience" as opposed to rote learning and direct instruction focused on the transmission of knowledge. However, Dewey most certainly did not advocate for pure "discovery learning," in which students are left to explore topics of their own choosing with minimal help from a teacher. He believed that the teacher should play an active role in guiding student learning—as do we, so we added seven "Project Based Teaching Practices" to our model of Gold Standard PBL. (For more information see the section to follow, "The Role of the Teacher in PBL.")

Need to know

A central concept in understanding Project Based Learning is that it creates a genuine "need to know" for students. That's the key to its motivating power. Instead of learning for the sake of getting a good grade or another extrinsic motivation, students in PBL learn because they're engaged by a project. They're emotionally invested in finding a solution to a real-world problem or an answer to a driving question that's relevant or important to them.

Main course, not dessert

Another key thing to understand about Project Based Learning is that the "project" is basically synonymous with the "unit" of instruction—or at least the central feature of a unit.

In a typical unit of instruction containing what many people call a "project," a teacher covers a topic with a combination of lectures, textbook readings, worksheets, and perhaps short activities, video programs and website visits. Then, students are given an assignment to do on their own at home: say, to create a poster about a disease, showing its effects on the body, how the body reacts, and how it is treated. These "projects" are displayed in the classroom, but are not formally presented or discussed in detail. The unit culminates with a test emphasizing factual recall.

As Ron Berger of EL Education first put it, the teacher covers the main content of the unit in the usual way, and then a short project is served up for "dessert." Visit a traditional classroom, and you'll probably find that students have done dessert projects in at least one unit during the school year. From shoebox dioramas to hand-built models to poster presentations to research reports, students are often tasked with creating something related to the topic of the unit. It's usually done near the end, or perhaps as a "side dish" during a unit, after the main course of content is delivered via traditional instruction.

In Project Based Learning, the project is the main course—it contains and frames the curriculum and instruction. The project itself is used to teach rigorous academic content and success skills.

What Is "Gold Standard" PBL?

In 2015, the Buck Institute for Education established a "gold standard" for Project Based Learning, building on its experience supporting PBL for over 20 years and drawing from an extensive research literature review. We did this to help ensure that PBL would be done well as its popularity increased, so it delivered on its promises and didn't become another one of yesterday's educational fads.

Our model for Gold Standard PBL has two parts: the seven Essential Project Design Elements, and the seven Project Based Teaching Practices.

In each part, the focus is on student learning goals—hence their placement in the center of the following figures. Student learning goals include academic knowledge and skills, and deep understanding of concepts and processes. Learning goals also include success skills such as critical thinking, problem-solving, collaboration, communication, creativity, and project management. This focus is meant to remind us that projects should be rigorous.

Essential Project Design Elements

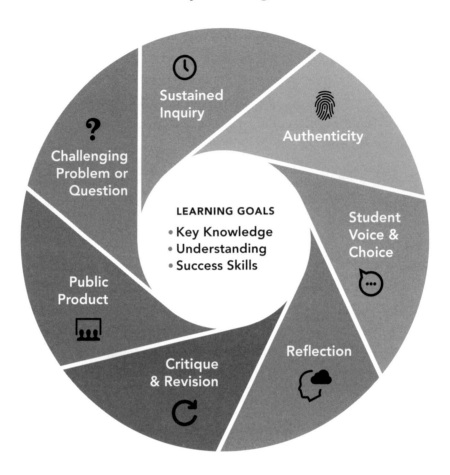

Challenging Problem or Question
The project is framed by a meaningful problem to solve or a question to answer, at the appropriate level of challenge.

Sustained Inquiry
Students engage in a rigorous, extended process of asking questions, finding resources, and applying information.

Authenticity
The project features real-world context, tasks and tools, quality standards, or impact—or speaks to students' personal concerns, interests, and issues in their lives.

Student Voice & Choice

Students make some decisions about the project, including how they work and what they create, and express their own ideas in their own voice.

Reflection

Students and teachers reflect on the effectiveness of their inquiry and project activities, the quality of student work, obstacles and how to overcome them.

Critique & Revision

Students give, receive, and use feedback to improve their process and products.

Public Product

Students make their project work public by sharing it with and explaining or presenting it to people beyond the classroom.

We'll say more about these elements in Chapter 1 "Designing and Planning a Project." It's important to note that the extent to which these elements are included in projects can vary. This is meant to be aspirational, not a seldomly-reached standard.

The High Quality PBL Framework

Our model for Gold Standard PBL aligns with the HQPBL Framework, which was created in 2017 through a collaborative effort by leading experts and PBL-focused organizations. The HQPBL Framework describes what students experience in a good project; our model describes what teachers do to get them there. Find out more at www.hqpbl.org.

PBL's Effectiveness: What We Know from the Research

There has been over 20 years of research on the kind of Project Based Learning we talk about in this book. As can always be said about education research, more needs to be done—and in recent years the pace and quality of research focused on PBL is increasing. Despite this progress, there is still lack of agreement about how to define PBL. Studying the effectiveness of PBL is challenging; there are many variables, including how well projects are designed, how well they are implemented by teachers, and the validity and reliability of measures.

In a 2018 PBLWorks research brief on PBL, "Project Based Learning and Student Achievement," PBLWorks Chief Impact Officer Dr. Sally Kingston put it this way:

"Research shows that PBL *can* promote student learning and may be more effective than traditional instruction in social studies, science, mathematics, and literacy. The 20 studies reviewed in this brief show that PBL can promote student learning in social studies and science; and, to a more limited degree, in mathematics and literacy."

We should note that there has been more research on problem-based learning than there is on the Gold Standard Project Based Learning we promote. However, we think the findings apply to both, since they're so similar (Larmer, 2013). The research has found that:

- Knowledge generated by completing authentic tasks is better organized and integrated with prior knowledge, seen as more meaningful by students, and applied more easily to new situations (Hung et al., 2007).
- Problem-based learning is more effective than traditional instruction in situations in which students have to use knowledge, not just remember it (Dochy et al., 2003; Strobel & van Barneveld, 2009).
- Students taught via problem-based learning remember what they're learned longer than those taught with traditional methods (Capon & Kuhn, 2004; Dochy et al., 2003).
- Project Based Learning promotes student engagement, because it involves student collaboration with peers, voice and choice, the completion of authentic work and its public display, and novelty (Blumenfeld et al., 1991; Brophy, 2013).

Three research studies are worth a special mention, because they (a) are recent, (b) focus on rigorous Project Based Learning, (c) are considered gold standard research as they involved high numbers of students and randomized control groups, and (d) have found very positive results for PBL on traditional test-based measures, for *all* subgroups of students. Here are their key findings:

2nd Grade Social Studies and Literacy:

The Impact of Project-Based Learning on Second Graders' Social Studies and Literacy Learning and Motivation in Low-SES School Settings (Duke, et al., 2020)

- PBL can raise student achievement in high-poverty communities.
- Gains made by the PBL group were 63% higher in social studies and 23% higher in informational reading than the control group.

3rd Grade Science and Social-Emotional Learning (SEL):

Project-Based Learning Increases Science Achievement in Elementary School and Advances Social and Emotional Learning (Krajcik et al., 2021).

- Third graders in PBL classrooms performed 8 percentage points better on a science assessment than students in traditional classrooms.
- The researchers "found this positive effect across schools with differing racial and ethnic makeups and household-income statuses and throughout the major regions of the state" (of Michigan).
- "Significant and positive effects" were found on social and emotional learning related to science learning. "Specifically, students more frequently reported the value of reflection and collaboration."

High School Advanced Placement Environmental Science and U.S. Government and Politics:

Knowledge in Action Efficacy Study Over Two Years (Saavedra et al., 2021. Funded by Lucas Education Research)

- Students taught with a PBL approach passed their AP tests at an 8% higher rate than students in traditionally taught classrooms. In the second year of the study the rate increased to 10%.
- Students from low-income households gained as much as higher-income students.

You can find more information and several published studies about PBL in the "Research" section at the PBLWorks.org website.

About John Hattie's Research

John Hattie, a widely-respected education researcher at the University of Melbourne, Australia, in his meta-analysis of many factors and strategies that impact student learning, found that "PBL"—meaning problem-based learning—had a negative impact. He found similar results for the broad category of "inquiry-based learning" generally. Many proponents of Project Based Learning have noticed that people who are wary of it cite Hattie's work.

We don't think Hattie's findings are incompatible with our model of PBL, however; here's why:

❯ Hattie looked at problem-based learning, not rigorous models of Project Based Learning such as Gold Standard PBL. Typical practice of problem-based learning (like the purer forms of "discovery learning" or inquiry-based learning) is more explicitly student-driven, with a much less active role for the teacher in providing instruction than the PBLWorks model.

❯ Hattie looked at studies conducted before 2005, which were primarily from post-secondary settings such as medical and nursing schools, where the problem-based learning model was first developed in the 1960s. Since 2005 more research has been done on "Project Based Learning" specifically, in K–12 settings—with promising results.

❯ Hattie found that problem-based learning, while not as effective for "accumulation of facts" (which is mainly what traditional testing measures) was indeed effective for "understanding the principles," application of knowledge, and improving retention of knowledge.

❯ Hattie did find high effect sizes for several practices that are, in fact, present in Gold Standard PBL, such as:

- High expectations
- Strong student-teacher relationships
- Frequent, helpful feedback
- Deliberate teaching of learning strategies

The Role of the Teacher in PBL

The chapters in this book are organized by the seven Project Based Teaching Practices in our model for Gold Standard PBL.

We decided to emphasize the concept of "project based teaching" to counter some stereotypes about PBL, such as: teachers just step back while students work independently on projects of their own choosing. There is a place for that kind of PBL, which is more often seen with older students. However, this book emphasizes projects that are facilitated and designed by teachers, or co-designed with students—and that involve student collaboration in teams, at least for part of the project. But even in independent student projects, there is a role for the teacher, as facilitator, resource-finder, monitor of progress, and content expert.

Another stereotype is that adopting PBL means teachers must abandon all their traditional teaching practices. No more direct instruction, lectures, textbooks, or worksheets. No quizzes or tests. There can, in fact, be a place for these tools and strategies within the context of a project. But they're employed judiciously, only if and when needed. For example, you could give a "mini-lecture" when students need to understand a particular concept or acquire a set of facts. Think of the project as the envelope that contains practices like those above as well as formative assessment, differentiation, discussions and workshops.

That said, the role of the teacher does change in a PBL environment. The metaphor "student as worker, teacher as coach" (Sizer, 1990) applies. When transitioning to PBL, one of the biggest hurdles for many teachers is the need to give up some degree of control over the classroom, and trust in their students. They are often the "guide on the side" instead of the "sage on the stage"—even though their subject-area and pedagogical expertise remain vital to the success of a project.

We should note that, when teachers and students are new to PBL, there is typically a need for more pre-planning and structured facilitation by the teacher. With more experience, students can work more independently, allowing for their age and capability, and even choose, with guidance, the focus of a project and what they will produce.

One more note: once teachers feel comfortable with PBL, they usually say they would "never go back" to traditional instruction. Their students are engaged and energized. They see how much their students gain, and enjoy their new role. Teachers we know even say PBL restores the "joy of teaching" to their work.

When you look at the seven teaching practices below, keep the above in mind. These practices might all be seen in a traditional classroom, but are reframed in the context of PBL.

Project Based Teaching Practices

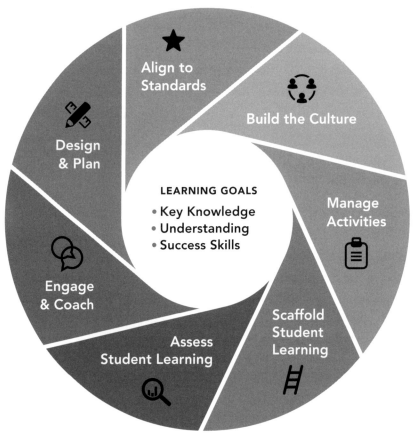

Design & Plan

Teachers create or adapt a project for their context and students, and plan its implementation from launch to culmination while allowing for student voice and choice.

Align to Standards

Teachers use standards to plan the project and make sure it addresses key knowledge and understanding from subject areas to be included.

Build the Culture

Teachers explicitly and implicitly promote student independence and growth, open-ended inquiry, team spirit, and attention to quality.

Manage Activities

Teachers work with students to organize tasks and schedules, set checkpoints and deadlines, find and use resources, create products and make them public.

Scaffold Student Learning

Teachers employ a variety of lessons, tools, and instructional strategies to support all students in reaching project goals.

Assess Student Learning

Teachers use formative and summative assessments of knowledge, understanding, and success skills, and include self- and peer-assessment of team and individual work.

Engage & Coach

Teachers engage in learning and creating alongside students, and identify when they need skill-building, redirection, encouragement, and celebration.

Equity and Project Based Learning

All students deserve PBL, and *can* do it successfully, with the right support. PBL can be transformative for students, especially those who are furthest from educational opportunity. PBL, when done with an intentional and culturally responsive mindset, can be a tool for equity.

These three statements capture the basic points we'd like to make about equity and PBL. Each could be a chapter unto themselves, so this is only a summary; we encourage you to find out more about equity and PBL in the references listed and on the PBLWorks website and its PBL blog.

All Students Can Do PBL

Which students should "get to have" the kind of learning experience PBL provides: Only students whose test scores are high enough? Only students who speak English fluently enough? Only students who are old enough or "well-behaved"? Only students in special schools or special programs, or in career/tech classes or electives but not core academic subjects?

Our answer would be "no" to all of the above. Let's tackle them one by one.

Test Scores

Traditionally, when students are judged to be "low skilled"—as measured by test scores, primarily—they are given direct instruction. Textbook assignments, lectures, worksheets, "packets," quizzes and tests. "Standards-aligned" lessons guided step-by-step by a teacher. Although most teachers do what they can to liven things up, it's not exactly an engaging way to teach and learn, nor is it as effective as its proponents hope (McTighe, 2017). It's even been called "drill and kill." It has also been called "the pedagogy of poverty" (Haberman, 1991) because students from lower-income families in urban schools are the ones who experience it most often. The same goes for too many students with special needs.

There's another inequity in this situation that has to do with the goals for students' education. Traditional instruction focuses mainly on imparting factual knowledge and basic skills. In today's economy, however—and life as a citizen in a democracy—everyone needs more than easily-searched-for information. Why should the success skills PBL provides opportunities to build, such as critical thinking, problem-solving, communication, collaboration, creativity, and project management, only be taught to certain students?

We should not withhold the good stuff from historically underserved groups of students or have low expectations for what they can do. Using PBL does not mean they are not being prepared for tests; there is even evidence that students taught via PBL do better on tests compared to those taught with traditional instruction (see the "PBL's Effectiveness" section of this introduction). Our model for Gold Standard PBL emphasizes designing and managing projects that align to standards, unlike the stereotype that PBL is "fun" but not academically rigorous.

Language Proficiency

The same could be said of students whose first language was not English. They deserve PBL too, not just direct instruction. It provides opportunities to practice speaking and listening skills in a real-world context and through team work with peers, as well as authentic reading and writing. This is not to say that there is no place for direct instruction when learning a language. PBL can be used along with traditional literacy programs for part of a school day or week, and skill-building lessons can be incorporated into a project. You'll find out more as you read this book.

Age or "Maturity" Level

Sometimes we hear teachers say, "PBL sounds great, but my kids couldn't handle it." They're too young. They're not mature enough, not capable of working on a team or independently from the teacher. They lack the necessary skills, habits, or mindset.

It's true that very young students need more support, but we've seen great examples of the successful use of PBL in the primary grades. The same is true for students with special needs—they can do PBL with the right amount of support. And it's true that many older students would not be "ready" for PBL if their whole experience of school had been sitting quietly in rows, listening to a teacher, following instructions, memorizing information and spitting it back on a test.

The transition from passive learner (who might also be turned off of school, period) to an active one who asks questions, finds resources, and produces high-quality work is not going to be made overnight. It might take time to establish a PBL-friendly culture and build the skills and habits needed for success with PBL. We'll say more about this in Chapter 3, "Building the Culture," and Chapter 6, "Scaffolding Student Learning."

Special Programs

PBL is often associated with special programs and special schools. Special programs go by many different names: applied learning classes, Gifted and Talented Education, design labs, maker spaces, "genius hours," and "passion project" time. Special schools include schools-within-schools, charter schools, and independent progressive schools—or PBL is developed at only one school in a district.

These kinds of programs are certainly beneficial to the students who experience them, so they have their place. And the special schools often have exemplary projects, structures, and practices others can learn from. But we believe PBL can and should be used in the "regular" program at regular schools—otherwise it will not reach many of the students who need it most. Likewise, PBL can and should be used in all subject areas, although its frequency and design might differ in say, a math class vs. a social studies class. The examples and guidance in this book will be drawn from all academic disciplines.

PBL Can Be Transformative for Students

Many students, especially Black and brown students, find school to be a dispiriting or even an oppressive place. Our education system replicates the inequity they face in a white-dominated society. The curriculum and instructional methods typically found in school do not speak to their cultures or identities. They may feel powerless both in school and in their lives.

Imagine the effect that PBL can have on these students. Imagine how empowering it can be to have successfully completed a project—or several projects, throughout their years in school—in which they identified and addressed a real-world problem in their community. In which they made their voice heard when answering a profound question that was important to them. In which they were recognized for doing high-quality work, by or even in collaboration with adults and experts from the world outside of school.

Students may also develop career interests from doing a project—and through PBL they gain the skills that will help them succeed in future education or on the job, from problem-solving to collaboration to project management to communication with diverse others.

PBL Aligns with Culturally Responsive Teaching

Culturally responsive teaching is a pedagogy that recognizes the importance of including students' cultural references in all aspects of learning (Ladson-Billings,1994). It has three dimensions: institutional (school organization, policies, procedures), personal (how teachers learn to be culturally responsive), and instructional, which is where PBL comes in.

Here's how culturally responsive teaching is reflected in PBL:

❱ When designing projects, building the classroom culture, and engaging and coaching students, PBL teachers honor and draw upon the "funds of knowledge" students bring from their homes.

❱ Key aspects of a PBL classroom culture include high expectations, a growth mindset, being a "warm demander," and an emphasis on high-quality work.

❱ PBL teachers vary teaching strategies, including ones that are preferred in some cultural groups, such as cooperative learning.

❱ Projects can focus on issues or concepts that involve or apply to the students' community or cultural group.

❱ Students are encouraged to direct their own learning in PBL, and work with other students.

(drawn from material by The Education Alliance, Brown University)

Remote Learning & PBL

In the spring of 2020, when schools closed their campuses during the Covid-19 pandemic, teachers noticed something, after they figured out how to use video conferencing and other tech tools to make remote learning possible. Many students were not engaged by traditional instruction that was simply moved online. They were not motivated to listen to lessons or lectures on their computer, complete online worksheets, and do textbook assignments. Not that many of them may have been engaged in the traditional classroom either, but it became even more apparent without the in-person appeal of a teacher or interaction with classmates.

Social-Emotional Learning and PBL

Many educators today are paying attention to students' social and emotional needs, in addition to academic needs. According to the Collaborative for Academic, Social and Emotional Learning (CASEL), "Social and emotional competencies can be taught, modeled, and practiced and lead to positive student outcomes that are important for success in school and in life." Furthermore, CASEL believes SEL "helps establish equitable learning environments."

CASEL has developed a framework for SEL with five "core competencies." Here's how they align with Project Based Learning, as shown in this table:

SEL Competencies:	Examples of the Competency also Seen in PBL:
1. Self-awareness: The abilities to understand one's own emotions, thoughts, and values and how they influence behavior across contexts.	**Students:** • Link feelings, values, and thoughts • Experience self-efficacy • Know that having a growth mindset is part of the classroom culture • Develop interests and sense of purpose
2. Self-management: The abilities to manage one's emotions, thoughts, and behaviors effectively in different situations and to achieve goals and aspirations.	• Use planning and organizational skills • Take initiative • Demonstrate personal and collective agency • Set personal and collective goals
3. Responsible decision-making: The abilities to make caring and constructive choices about personal behavior and social interactions across diverse situations.	• Are encouraged to be curious and open-minded • Learn to make reasoned judgment with information, data, facts • Identify solutions for problems • Recognize usefulness of critical thinking skills
4. Relationship skills: The abilities to establish and maintain healthy and supportive relationships and to effectively navigate settings with diverse individuals and groups.	• Learn to communicate effectively • Practice teamwork and collaborative problem-solving • Show leadership in groups • Seek or offer support and help when needed
5. Social awareness: The abilities to understand the perspectives of and empathize with others, including those from diverse backgrounds, cultures, and contexts.	• Take others' perspectives • Recognize strengths in others • Demonstrate empathy and compassion • Recognize situational demands and opportunities

Source: www.casel.org

On the other hand, we heard many reports from teachers who used PBL for remote learning who noticed their students *were* still engaged. They were showing up for meetings, communicating with teachers, and using tech tools with their peers— and interested in tackling real-world topics and solving problems relevant to their communities and lives. Not all projects can work for remote learning, but many can, with the right adaptations, tools, and strategies.

Project Based Learning makes sense for remote or hybrid learning environments. Here are four reasons why:

1. Many of the practices used in PBL are relatively easy to convert to an online environment, such as whole-group meetings followed by breakout groups, critique protocols, discussion boards, and project management strategies. Students and teachers might already be familiar with using tech tools to manage their work, collaborate and communicate, and create products.

2. Projects that are authentic to real-world issues and relevant to students' lives are inherently motivating. The problems and ongoing issues faced by our nation and the world—from pandemics to income inequality to racial justice to climate change—provide many opportunities for such projects. Not every project can be adapted for the online environment—for example, if it centers on a team-created tangible product or a particular physical location—but many can.

3. In PBL, the teacher does not control everything that goes on in the classroom. A PBL culture emphasizes independent student work time, collaboration with a team, and inquiry guided by students' questions. This translates well to at-home learning where the teacher (much less a parent or caregiver who needs to work) is not able to observe and guide students as frequently as they can in a classroom.

4. One of the key aspects of authenticity in PBL is a connection with audiences, experts, and organizations beyond the classroom. Students working on projects at home, already working online and using tech tools for communication and collaboration, find it easier and more natural to make these connections than they often do in brick and mortar schools.

Here's another reason PBL is a good idea for remote learning: it provides social-emotional support for students, which is especially needed during uncertain times and disruptions of students' lives. As PBLWorks's Laureen Adams said in a blog post, "Now, more than ever, it is imperative that we foster a humanizing pedagogy. Students need to feel safe, cared for, and seen" (Adams, 2020).

The Project Based Teaching Practices in our model for Gold Standard PBL reflect this imperative, especially "Build the Culture" and "Engage and Coach." Effective PBL teachers cultivate relationships with students; they get to know them well so they can design relevant projects and act as a "warm demander" (see more on this role in Chapter 7, "Engaging and Coaching Students"). They build on students' strengths, uncovering their existing funds of knowledge (Maitra, 2016). They pay attention to what students are going through and the challenges they face, stepping in to offer support when needed, and include frequent supportive feedback throughout a project.

You'll find "For Remote Learning" sidebars in chapters of this book with more information and advice, including helpful tech tools, for using PBL in remote learning.

Why PBL Is Right for Students of This Age

We'll conclude this introduction with some thoughts on why Project Based Learning is appropriate for students of middle school and high school age.

PBL is appropriate for tweens and early teens because it involves:

Independent learning

The tween and early-teen brain is said to be "all accelerator and no brake," so once you engage them, you just need to get out of their way (as much as possible).

Self-reflection

Students of this age are beginning to reflect on who they are and who they are becoming. They're getting their first phone, perhaps a job, spending more time away from their families, and figuring out their identities. In PBL, they are asked to reflect on who they are as learners and team members, on their goals and interests, and on what issues and questions they would like to investigate.

Choice

Learning how to make their own choices is how tweens and early-teens begin to prepare for independent learning, thinking, and life. Just as this might be the time in a student's life when they are given a key to the apartment, so is this the time to allow students choice and direction in how and what to learn. Being allowed to make choices in PBL helps young people learn how to make good decisions—and with teacher guidance, a student can be redirected without the journey being too high-risk yet.

Collaboration

A major part of a middle schooler's life is social; it's about talking, or being scared to talk. If we isolate them in the learning process, they can't bounce ideas off each other, vent with each other, and seek advice from peers; we are cutting them off from their very life-blood. On the flipside, tweens and early teens who are socially awkward (and let's face it, that's many of them) need collaboration skills to grow both academically and socially. If students have difficulty working with others, that's the teacher's signal to "up the ante" by requiring it in a project—with the right scaffolding of course.

Making an impact

With PBL, young people see that they can make an impact on the world around them. Many elementary students still look to their parents to make decisions for them and don't see themselves as having any power. High schoolers are given opportunities to sit on committees with adults, do volunteer work, support a cause, and even vote. Middle schoolers, on the other hand, feel they are ready to be handed the reins of decision-making but don't know what to do with them. PBL helps in that training.

Broadening a student's experience

Middle school, more than any other part of K–12 education, is about exploration. Tweens and early teens are old enough to begin making more of their own choices about their lives. They begin considering potential careers or how their interests and talents could translate into real-world pursuits. By the time they are in high school, students may begin solidifying these plans, but middle school offers flexibility for discovering things. Middle school, in a sense, is their "last chance" to explore, and PBL offers exceptional opportunities for acting in real-world roles and learning how professionals solve problems and create useful products and ideas.

Questioning

Tweens and early teens are becoming more oppositional or skeptical of authority. Unlike younger students, they expect to be told "why" before complying with teacher directions or requests. While this can be frustrating for a teacher, it can be leveraged and focused on curiosity, inquiry, and evidence-based discussions, all features of PBL. Moreover, an engaging, authentic project provides the answer to "why" they need to learn or do something.

Most of the above reasons apply to older teens too. In addition, PBL is good for high school students because it involves:

Preparation for post-secondary options

All students deserve the opportunity to engage in rigorous and engaging curriculum in school, and this is particularly important as high school students begin to think about their post-secondary journeys. Providing students with the opportunity to apply learning to real-world contexts, model the work often done in the professional world, and answer deep, nuanced questions will help them identify their passions, interests, and strengths as students and individuals.

Building skills and personal qualities needed for college

In college, students not only need to bring a certain amount of disciplinary knowledge; they need to be independent learners who can manage themselves. They need to know more than how to listen to lectures, take notes, and cram for exams. The skills PBL teaches will serve them well, from knowing how to work with others, make presentations, and manage long-term projects. We've even heard that high school graduates who've had a lot of PBL under their belt feel more comfortable and inclined to approach their professors, a time-honored marker of success in college, because they're used to working with their teachers as coaches and partners in learning (Rey, 2017).

Building skills needed for the workplace

In the modern workplace, people need more than basic knowledge of reading, writing, and arithmetic (with a bit of science, history, and appreciation for literature thrown in), which the over-century-old "factory model" of schooling was designed to teach. Today, people on the job need to know much more: how to solve problems, find creative solutions, work in teams, communicate with diverse others, manage projects, and provide leadership. PBL is highly effective for learning and practicing these kinds of success skills.

Learning what citizenship means

Teenagers who already are or soon will be eligible to vote, join organizations, and serve their communities can, by engaging in authentic projects, learn how important it is to actively participate in a democracy. They can find issues they care about and develop opinions and beliefs—and the capacity to think well—that will last a lifetime.

Addressing real issues and problems

Teenagers today are all-too-aware of the many problems facing our society and the world—and they want to do something about them. Projects can engage them in identifying and addressing issues that are important to them, from personal to local to global.

Before We Continue

Look for these special features as you read this book:

PBL PRO TIP   Advice from veteran PBL teachers.

FOR REMOTE LEARNING

Notes on how to implement projects in remote or blended/hybrid settings, including helpful technology tools.

Sidebars and Special Pages

You'll see these scattered throughout the book, with information on topics that require special attention.

Ready to learn more about how to design Gold Standard PBL projects and implement them successfully? Read on!

CHAPTER 1

Designing and Planning a Project

DESIGNING AND PLANNING A PROJECT IS FUN —and it also takes some work. It requires time, because you're basically creating a whole unit of instruction, not just a few lessons. Don't be daunted, though. You can start with a relatively simple project, and progress toward more ambitious ones later. You will also find that you'll be able to use many of the teaching practices and even some lessons and materials you already use—you'll just need to reframe them in the context of PBL.

The more experience you have with PBL, the easier it is to design and plan projects. You'll understand the essential elements of a good project, know some shortcuts, and have a better sense of what you can leave up to your students or handle as you go along. When you're just starting out, though, allow plenty of time for this step in the process and plan thoroughly.

One more note about planning and the "time" issue that often comes up for teachers who want to use PBL: the time you spend planning up front gives you more time *during* the project. With a solid plan going in, you'll find when the project is being implemented that you'll have the time to be more responsive to students. Compared to the often-rushed pace of preparing and delivering daily lessons in traditional instruction, the time in a project will feel more meaningful and sometimes relaxed and even "spacious."

"Design & Plan" in the Project Based Teaching Rubric:

❯ Project includes all Essential Project Design Elements as described on the Project Design Rubric.

❯ Detailed and accurate plans include scaffolding and assessing student learning and a project calendar, which remains flexible to meet student needs.

❯ Resources for the project have been anticipated to the fullest extent possible and arranged well in advance.

The Project Planner

In the appendix of this book is a document, the Project Planner, also available at PBLWorks.org. This chapter will explain how to think about the Planner's four sections:

Project Overview
The basic idea for the project, driving question, major products, and time frame.

Learning Goals
Targeted standards, key vocabulary, literacy skills, and success skills.

Project Milestones
Significant moments or stages, usually with formative assessment.

Project Calendar
Day-to-day activities in the project.

Take an Easier Route? Adapting an Existing Project

Although this chapter talks about designing your own project from scratch, you might want to take an easier route and find a project designed by someone else. This can save time and help ensure the quality of a project, IF the project is well-designed—meaning it features the seven Essential Project Design Elements in Gold Standard PBL. So check it carefully to see if you need to add or strengthen certain elements. And read this chapter anyway, so you understand what to look for and how to plan the implementation details!

Note that even if you find a good project, you will need to make tweaks so it will engage and benefit your particular students, and work for you:

❯ Consider your students (their strengths, needs, interests, prior knowledge, cultural backgrounds, abilities, language skills, etc.).

❯ Consider your context (material and human resources in the community and school, schedules, weather, potential partners, authentic connections to community issues, etc.).

❯ Consider your content (standards, graduate profile outcomes, pacing guides, student prior knowledge, curriculum resources— what you need to teach and what your students will need in order to learn it).

There are many sources of projects available, and one of the best is the project library at pblworks.org. Check out their "Project Designer" tool for adapting the projects.

Essential Project Design Elements

To begin, let's go over the seven Essential Project Design Elements in the PBLWorks model for Gold Standard PBL in more detail. Keep all of them in mind as you design and plan a project. We'll be referring to them in this and other chapters in this book. In the appendix you can find a complete Project Design Rubric, which describes a project that includes all these elements to a high degree, a project that includes them but needs further development, and a project that lacks these features. The table on the next page shows the indicators for the highest level.

Project Design Rubric

Essential Project Design Element	Indicator
Challenging Problem or Question	• The project is focused on a central problem or question, at the appropriate level of challenge. • The project is framed by a driving question, which is: – open-ended; there is more than one possible answer – understandable and inspiring to students – aligned with learning goals; to answer it, students will need to gain the intended knowledge, understanding, and skills
Sustained Inquiry	• Inquiry is sustained over time and academically rigorous (students pose questions, gather & interpret data, develop and evaluate solutions or build evidence for answers, and ask further questions). • Inquiry is driven by student-generated questions throughout the project.
Authenticity	• The project has an authentic context, involves real-world tasks, tools, and quality standards, makes an impact on the world, and/or speaks to students' personal concerns, interests, or identities.
Student Voice & Choice	• Students have opportunities to express their voice and make choices on important matters (topics to investigate, questions asked, texts and resources used, people to work with, products to be created, use of time, organization of tasks). • Students have opportunities to take significant responsibility and work as independently from the teacher as is appropriate, with guidance.
Reflection	• Students and teachers engage in thoughtful, comprehensive reflection both during the project and after its culmination, about what and how students learn and the project's design and management.
Critique & Revision	• Students are provided with regular, structured opportunities to give and receive feedback about the quality of their products and work-in-progress from peers, teachers, and if appropriate from others beyond the classroom. • Students use feedback about their work to revise and improve it.
Public Product	• Student work is made public by presenting, displaying, or offering it to people beyond the classroom. • Students are asked to explain the reasoning behind choices they made, their inquiry process, how they worked, what they learned, etc.

Planning a Project: Different Ways to Start

Teachers often ask a chicken-or-egg question when designing a project: Do I start with my curriculum/standards, or with an idea that's going to engage my students? The answer could go either way. Sometimes an idea, a driving question, or a product to be created will just come to you (or students), then you decide what learning goals to align the project to.

At other times, you might start with the learning goals for students to meet, then think of a project in which students could demonstrate their achievement of them. We'll say more about this approach in Chapter 2, "Aligning to Standards."

Let's talk first about getting ideas for projects, which can come from a variety of sources of inspiration:

- **An existing unit in your curriculum that you can re-envision as a project**
  Perhaps there's a unit in your course that students find particularly interesting—or not so interesting and in need of livening up—that could be turned into a project by adding one or more Essential Project Design Elements. For example, think about how the content might connect to an authentic problem or public product.

- **A real-world issue in your community (or beyond it) that students can help address**
  Sometimes these can fall into your lap: a pandemic; a rise in bullying at school; pollution in a local waterway; protests over social justice issues. Or, you and your students can seek out problems: homelessness in the community; local businesses need help with marketing themselves; a need to reduce the amount of waste produced by households and businesses. You could also partner with a nonprofit organization to help with a problem they're trying to address.

- **Current events, popular culture, and your students' interests**
  Lots of possibilities here—the key is knowing your students. Find out what social media, technology, websites, books, TV, movies, and music they like. Talk with them or give them a survey to find out what issues they're grappling with in their lives. If there's a big story in the news, figure out what students could or would like to do in response.

- **A problem faced by professionals that your students can tackle**

  This could be an actual problem or a situation that replicates one. For example, students could design a bridge for a specific location, under constraints such as cost, capacity, and safety. Or, they could produce public service announcements or create a social media campaign to help their city government improve recycling. Connect with people in your family and community to learn about what they do in their jobs—these conversations can be rich and sometimes surprising sources of project ideas!

- **Your own passions and interests**

  In addition to your students' interests, your own could serve as the spark for a project. Perhaps you're dedicated to social justice in our society and want to take action on an issue. Maybe you're a reader of fan fiction, so you could get students engaged in writing and publishing it on a website. Or you love sports, and could hook students on a math project that compares stats on players and teams to predict who will win a season. Just be careful to NOT "make it all about you"—students have to own the project, so if they're not already excited about something, find ways to engage them, or find another topic.

Types of Projects

Here's another way to look at the possibilities for projects. As long as they include the Essential Project Design Elements, good projects can take many different forms. Here are five types, with examples from the PBLWorks project library:

Exploration of a philosophical question
- In the "Voices of the Revolution" project, students create podcasts that explore the question, Did the American Revolution have more than two sides? They consider the perspective of colonial leaders and the British and also the French, indigenous people, enslaved Africans, and members of various social classes in the colonies.
- In the "Face Your Face" project, students explore the question, What masks do we wear when we go about our daily lives? They learn about masks in various world cultures and their purposes, then create their own masks.

Designing Projects *with* Students, Not *for* Them

Many experienced PBL teachers like to involve students in designing and planning projects. This builds a sense of ownership that can propel students to do high-quality work they're passionate about—which makes for a powerful learning experience.

Students can be involved in designing and planning projects in a range of ways:

- Co-writing a driving question after an entry event
- Exploring a topic introduced by the teacher to see what piques their interest
- Seeking out problems to solve in their community
- Identifying current events, cultural trends, or important issues in their lives that could be the focus of a project
- Planning the process by which they will complete the project (a good way to teach project management skills)
- Deciding on major products and how to make them public

Investigation of a historical event, time period, or natural phenomenon

- In the "Golden Age" project, students create museum exhibits that answer the question, What lessons can we learn from golden age civilizations and/or from their falls, and why do those lessons matter to us today?

- In the "A Brief History of Several Billion Years" project, students address the question, How did the continents come to look the way they do, and how will they change in the future? They work with staff from a natural history museum or nature education center to develop a physical time line and an interactive virtual museum exhibit.

Problem-solving situation

- In the "Grow it Green" project, students design an experiment to compare traditional vs. hydroponic methods for growing vegetables as they answer the driving question, How can we reduce the impact of our food-growing systems on the environment?

- In the "Broken Laws" projects, students draft a proposal for a new law or an amendment to an existing law (proposition or legislation) and take action to get the law passed or changed at the local, state, or federal level.

Examination of a controversial issue
- In the "Community Voices" project, students address the question, How can we use data to tell a local story that will inform and motivate community members to action?
- In the "Climate: The Change We Need" project, students learn about causes and effects of climate change and create infographics that use data to tell a local story that will inform and motivate community members to action.

Challenge to design, plan, or create something
- In the "Mysteries, Solved!" project, students develop and publish mystery stories in the form of written texts or graphic novels, then share these stories in a community event.
- In the "The Many Functions of Walking" project, students plan a walk-a-thon in order to raise money for a cause or event that is important to their community.
- In the "Making Space for Change" project, students create an environmentally sustainable redesign for a community space, such as a park, library, public square, empty lot, or community center.

Re: authenticity and simulations

To design a project that's "authentic," think broadly about what that word means. A project can be authentic in several ways, often in combination. It can involve the use of real-world processes, tasks and tools, and performance standards, such as when students plan an experimental investigation or use digital editing software to produce videos approaching professional quality. A project can have personal authenticity when it speaks to students' own concerns, interests, cultures, identities, and issues in their lives. Often, the most impactful projects on students are the ones that are authentic because they have a real impact on other people, such as when students address a need in their school or community, or create something that will be used or experienced by others.

A project could also have an authentic context, such as when students solve problems like those faced by people in the world outside of school (e.g., entrepreneurs developing a business plan, engineers designing a bridge, or lawyers arguing a case). This type of authenticity leaves room for simulations, which may be just fine (or all you can do) for certain topics. For example, some classic civics projects fall into this category: the "Mock Trial," "Mock Legislature," and "Mock Election." Or students could play a role, such as advisors to the president recommending policy, consultants advising a corporation on how to make their product more environmentally friendly, or architects proposing designs for tiny houses.

PBL PRO TIP

Make Sure Your Idea Is "Project-Worthy"

Before you settle on your project idea and begin developing your project, seek feedback from colleagues and perhaps even from students, to be sure the idea is "project-worthy." Ask, is it authentic and relevant to students? Will it sustain their interest over the duration of the project? Will students gain enough important knowledge and skills?

Setting Learning Goals

In the center of our diagrams of the Essential Project Design Elements and Project Based Teaching Practices are the student learning goals. They're in the center for a reason. Like the focus of the lens of a camera, the learning goals are the whole point of the project and the teaching.

Here are three types of learning goals we emphasize when designing a project:

Key knowledge

These goals could be drawn from your district, state, or national content standards and curriculum guides, or they could be based on your own expertise in a subject area. The key word is "key"—projects should focus on the really important standards in a particular academic discipline, sometimes called "priority" standards because they appear more often on high-stakes tests. (See more on selecting standards for projects in Chapter 2, "Aligning to Standards.")

Most of the content standards recently adopted by states in the U.S. today are about more than factual knowledge—they emphasize deeper understanding, disciplinary thinking, and real-world application. This is true for the Common Core State Standards for mathematics and literacy, the C3 Framework for Social Studies, and the Next Generation Science Standards—which include connections to engineering, as true STEM instruction should. These kinds of standards align well with PBL, so look to them when selecting learning goals for projects. For example:

CCSS Standards of Mathematical Practice; 4. Model with mathematics:
Mathematically proficient students can apply the mathematics they know to solve problems arising in everyday life, society, and the workplace.

College, Career, and Civic Life (C3) Framework for Social Studies State Standards; Four dimensions of informed inquiry:
1. Developing questions and planning inquiries; 2. Applying disciplinary concepts and tools; 3. Evaluating sources and using evidence; and 4. Communicating conclusions and taking informed action

Next Generation Science Standards; Practices of science and engineering:
1. Asking questions (for science) and defining problems (for engineering)… 3. Planning and carrying out investigations… 6. Constructing explanations (for science) and designing solutions (for engineering) 7. Engaging in argument from evidence 8. Obtaining, evaluating, and communicating information

Understanding

Goals for understanding can also be drawn from content standards and curriculum guides, or from your own knowledge and expertise. For projects, focus on important concepts, those that are central to the subject area or course. They should be deep, complex, and meant to stay with students for a long time. These goals are sometimes called "enduring understandings" that frame the "big ideas" in a discipline, that give meaning and are of lasting importance (Wiggins & McTighe, 2012). Here are some examples:

- *English Language Arts:* Great literature explores universal themes of human existence and can reveal truths through fiction.
- *Mathematics:* Quantitative data can be collected, organized, and displayed in a variety of ways. Mathematical ideas can be represented numerically, graphically, or symbolically.
- *Science:* The structures of materials determine their properties.
- *Social Studies:* The geography, climate, and natural resources of a region influence the culture, economy, and lifestyle of its inhabitants.

- *Arts/Humanities:* The relationship between the arts and culture is mutually dependent; culture affects the arts, and the arts reflect and preserve culture.

Success skills

Factual knowledge and conceptual understanding, by themselves, are not enough in today's world. In school and college, in the modern workplace, and as citizens and in their lives generally, people need to be able to think critically and solve problems, work well with others, communicate with diverse people, think creatively and innovatively, and manage their work effectively. We call these kinds of competencies "success skills," and they have also been known as "21st century skills," "school-wide outcomes," or "college and career readiness skills."

These competencies typically appear on school and district vision statements or where they describe their "graduate profile." However, what is often lacking is the connection to instructional practice, and that's where PBL comes in. It's the perfect vehicle for learning and practicing these skills. Without an explicit focus on developing success skills, including ways to assess and document their growth, schools cannot be sure they are actually being learned by students. They remain only as hopes without a plan, only words on a wall.

When designing a project, explicitly target success skills—but not too many, or you won't be able to teach them all and students won't really know what to focus on. For some projects you might emphasize only one or two for specific instruction and assessment, even though more are being practiced by students. Map out your success skills as you plan projects for a year or a course. For example, some projects naturally lend themselves to learning how to use creativity and a process for innovation. Other projects, perhaps early in the school year or in a course, could focus on how to think critically, a skill which could then be reinforced in projects to come. The same might also be true of communication and collaboration skills.

Before moving on, we should note that there are other kinds of learning goals that you may want to think about when designing a project. This might include things like "habits of mind" such as persisting, thinking flexibly, taking responsible risks, questioning, and problem posing (Costa & Kallick, 2008). Other goals could be based on what you personally value, or drawn from school or district mission/vision statements—goals like developing cross-cultural competency, global awareness, and democratic citizenship, to name a few. While you may not explicitly teach and assess these goals, students can still reflect on them and document their development.

Including Literacy in Every Project

No matter what you teach, every project you design and facilitate should help students build their literacy skills. Literacy includes listening, speaking, reading, and writing, and can look different in different content areas and disciplines. In order to design effective literacy supports in your project, consider the following questions:

What literacy practices are core to the discipline I am teaching, are used by professionals in related fields, or are relevant to the project context?

If you are a math teacher with a project on compound interest and financial literacy, have students practice reading, analyzing, and writing financial reports and data visualizations, and engage in discussions and presentations in which they explain their mathematical thinking. If you are a science teacher doing a project about climate change, students might practice reading scientific reports, sets of data, and news articles about the topic.

What skills will students need in order to access content or produce strong products for this project?

Consider the texts and resources students will engage with during the project. If they will be reading primary sources in history or theatrical scripts, consider the skills they will need to learn in order to make meaning of these texts. If students are producing podcasts, writing proposed legislation, or developing user guides, what will they need to learn in order to create products that are high-quality and relevant to the audience and purpose?

How will you teach literacy skills throughout the project?

As you plan your project calendar, make time to explicitly teach (and formatively assess) the literacy skills you are targeting. This might include introducing and practicing relevant vocabulary, analyzing "mentor texts" with students to explore specific attributes of a genre or text type, providing graphic organizers and checklists to help students plan and revise their written work and their presentations, and/or teaching mini-lessons on specific reading, writing, listening, or speaking strategies.

Planning an Interdisciplinary/Multi-Subject Project

Many of its practitioners think the ultimate Project Based Learning experience is interdisciplinary. Most real-world challenges or issues are, after all, too complex to be addressed from only one angle—from climate change to racial injustice to redesigning a local park in a community. This vision of PBL features a team of teachers in different disciplines, all working together on the same project with a shared cohort of students.

This kind of interdisciplinary PBL is great, and we hope it happens regularly in middle and high school. It's not without its hurdles, though. One is the traditional structure of secondary schools, with separate classrooms for different subjects, a six-period day, and student scheduling that doesn't allow for shared cohorts. Another is the difficulty of aligning the curricula in various subjects, to make sure a project's learning goals are important for each discipline and can be taught in the same time frame. A third is the time it takes for teachers to meet and plan a project together—rewarding as it is.

If you teach in a non-traditionally structured school, these challenges can be met. Many middle schools combine ELA, social studies, and perhaps the arts into one "humanities" course and have a "math/science" block. Some schools have created career academies or new courses such as "American Studies" or "Health Science" where interdisciplinary, team-taught projects work well. These courses typically combine time for whole-cohort project work with some separate time for specific subject-area lessons/support.

Consider the range of possible ways to include multiple subject areas in a project, even if it's not the ultimate in "interdisciplinarity." Combining two subjects and teaching with one other teacher might be just fine for some projects. Even if you're on your own, a project in a math, CTE, or science class will include some reading, writing, and speaking, so literacy is going to be embedded. Only certain English Language Arts projects might be called "single-subject" because they involve only literacy standards—for example publishing a book of student poetry (but if you include illustrations or graphic design, then arts standards are in there too!).

Here is some guidance on bringing multiple subject areas together in PBL:

- If you are doing a project on your own, include literacy, math, or the arts to the extent you can. Perhaps a colleague with expertise in those subjects could help you plan, or support students to a limited extent during the project by visiting your classroom as a guest expert or providing scaffolding or feedback on their work.

- If you are planning and conducting an interdisciplinary project with a team of colleagues, map out your curriculum and standards to look for connections. Use sticky notes to jot down the major topics/standards in each subject area and move them around on a whiteboard.

- If you and your colleagues do not share the same cohort of students, create a project with a driving question that can be answered in each subject area. Decide what parts of the project can be done separately in each classroom, and how they will be combined near the end.

Here are two common pitfalls to avoid:

Pitfall #1: One subject area is only "dessert."

In projects involving 3-4 subjects, one subject might be artificially tacked on. For example, having students create a pretty piece of visual art related to a project's topic can be superficial and devalues art as its own, meaningful subject. Another common example is when the math teacher only helps students interpret the statistical data in a science or history project. This sometimes happens in "STEM" programs, when one or two of those subjects are not included meaningfully in projects.

To avoid this situation, ensure that all subject areas involved have deep, meaningful content related to the project. If this cannot work for a particular project, have the subject that was less involved take the lead on the next project. Or, rethink how many subjects need to be brought together—perhaps some projects need only include two.

Pitfall #2: The "project" is more like a theme, with no shared product.
There may be value in having a theme (such as "change" or "helping our community") that is shared across subject areas, or even a whole grade level for certain curriculum units or periods of time. However, unless major products are also shared, it won't feel like "a project" and students may miss the connection.

To avoid this situation, make sure it does feel like one project. Launch the project together, with one entry event and driving question. Do the tough work of occasionally combining classes, planning an assembly, or trading rooms for a day so students see all teachers involved talking about the same thing in the same room. Actively use work done in the other classes in your own room. Do peer critique in your class about a product created in another class. Use the same materials and have common texts, pictures, and other artifacts visible in both classes.

Finally, and perhaps most obviously, finish the project together. Share in the exhibition of student work, and assess the work together (using shared rubrics). Have students reflect across subject areas, explicitly noting the ways they deepened their knowledge through interdisciplinary work.

For an example of how a teacher guides students to see connections between seemingly different real-world problems at the launch of a project, see the blog post by educator and author Michael McDowell, "Using PBL to Encourage Interdisciplinary Work" (Edutopia, 2020).

Find examples of interdisciplinary projects in the project library at PBLWorks.org.

Writing a Driving Question

The first Essential Project Design Element in Gold Standard PBL is "Challenging Problem or Question." It's important to capture the project's main focus in student-friendly language, so they're very clear on what the overall goal is. We like to use a "driving question" to accomplish this. The driving question is used throughout a project as a touchstone for students and a tool to guide their inquiry process. A driving question also helps you as the teacher, by focusing your planning on the knowledge, skills, and activities students will need in order to answer the driving question.

Writing a driving question may feel familiar to you if you are used to crafting essential questions in Understanding by Design or using problem/goal statements in design thinking.

PBL PRO TIP

Co-Create a Driving Question with Students

Some PBL teachers, for some projects, prefer to write the driving question with their students after the launch of a project. This honors students' thinking, teaches them how to ask "open-ended" questions, and helps build ownership of the project. See Chapter 7, "Engaging and Coaching Students," for more on how to do this.

A good driving question meets the following 3 criteria:

1. **Engaging for students**
   - Students can understand it, and it sounds provocative, intriguing, or important.
   - It is appropriate for students of the project's intended age, demographic background, community, and so on.
   - It does not sound like a typical question from a teacher or a textbook.
   - It leads students to ask further questions and begin the inquiry process.
   - Depending on the project, it might have a local context or a charge to take action, making it even more engaging.
   - When applicable, it uses the words "I," "we," or "us"—not "you" or "students"—to create a sense of ownership in students.

2. **Open-ended**
   - It has several possible answers, and the answer will be original; it is not "google-able" by students.
   - The answer is complex, requiring information-gathering and critical thinking.
   - It may be a question with a yes or no answer, but it must require a detailed explanation or justification.

3. **Aligned with learning goals**
   - To answer it, students will need to learn the project's targeted knowledge and understanding, and practice key success skills.
   - It does not simply restate the targeted content standard(s), but may contain language from standards if it does not make the question too lengthy or uninviting to students.
   - It is not too big, requiring more knowledge than can be learned in a reasonable amount of time (e.g., Who was the best U.S. president? or How might global warming affect life on Earth?).

We've noticed over the years of facilitating PBL workshops that one of the most challenging steps for teachers when designing a project is writing the driving question. Many teachers are great at creating curriculum units and lesson plans, and many are great at working with students, but crafting the wording of a question that captures the heart of a project and engages learners can be tricky.

We see two general types of driving questions in PBL, each with pros and cons.

Driving questions that explore a philosophical or debatable issue, or an intriguing topic, such as:

- Is there "liberty and justice for all" in our society?
- Could there be life on other planets?
- What should be our nation's policy on immigration?
- Should we be eating meat?
- Does our childhood make us who we are?
- What's the true cost of things we buy?
- What masks do we wear in our daily lives?

PROS: Highly engaging to students; the kind of question they'll keep talking about when they leave the classroom. Captures big ideas, important questions, and sounds inherently interesting.

CONS: Harder to write; may feel like advanced PBL practice because the task and product are not spelled out. May be more appropriate in certain subject areas (e.g., humanities, social studies) than others (e.g., math, world languages, career/tech). Younger students or English Language Learners may need support for understanding questions that are more abstract (e.g., the "masks" example above).

Driving questions that specify a product to be created or a problem to be solved—to which the students' role may be added, such as:
- How can we help protect an endangered species in our area?
- How can we reduce bullying?
- How can we design tiny houses that meet the needs of our community?
- How can we create a guide to our community for new immigrants?
- How can we, as historians, create podcasts that tell the story of our city?
- How can we, as medical interns, diagnose a sick patient?
- How can we use poetry to promote social justice in our community?

PROS: Easier to write. Authentic to how problems are solved and products are created in real-world situations. Helps focus younger students on their task in a project. Roles define the kind of thinking we want students to do (as historians, scientists, etc.), add a real-world element, and can be good for career exploration.

CONS: Can feel less engaging for students; sometimes simply states what the teacher wants students to do. Roles may feel fake to some students; older students especially may prefer being themselves.

Troubleshooting common pitfalls

The table on the next page shows some typical "first drafts" of driving questions and how they can be improved to better meet the above criteria.

First Draft Driving Question for PBL Unit	Critique	Revised Driving Question for PBL Unit
What adaptations do animal species make to survive in various habitats?	Not engaging, because it sounds like a teacher or textbook.	Could a dog live in the desert?
How can children's stories be written effectively?	Not as engaging as it could be; livelier language and a local focus would improve it.	How can we make stories come alive for kids in our community?
How is math used in basketball statistics?	Not engaging enough: too broad, not provocative.	Is LeBron James the best basketball player ever?
Which buildings in our county should be classified as historic and protected, because they represent important pieces of our past?	Not engaging, because it uses adult language and suggests the preferred answer.	Does it matter if old buildings in our county are torn down?
Should natural areas be developed?	Not as engaging as it would be if it were specific and local.	Should our city build new housing on the land near the river?
What were the causes of the U.S. Civil War?	Not open-ended and does not require critical thinking and debate.	What was the most important cause of the U.S. Civil War?
How do movies differ from the books on which they are based?	Not as engaging as it could be; adding "which is better?" makes it more so.	Which is better, the book or the movie?
What should people consider when planning for financing college or buying a home?	Not as engaging as it would be if it were specific and had a charge to take action.	What financial planning advice would we give to our "client" family so that they can make good decisions?
Why is genetic engineering a bad idea?	Engaging, but slanted in one direction.	Should we allow designer babies?
How can we use measurement skills and geometry to plan a park?	States learning goals but doesn't have to; lacks a purpose or "why."	How can we plan a park that people in our community will visit?
How can we, as filmmakers, create a public service announcement about protecting the health of babies?	Acceptable, but could be improved by adding a "so that" or criteria for success.	How can we, as filmmakers, create a public service announcement about protecting the health of babies that will have an impact on people?

Deciding on Major Products and How They Will Be Made Public

In PBL, students actually *create* something, as opposed to what happens in much of traditional instruction, where the focus is often on simply retaining information for a test or completing an assignment. And what students create in a project is shared publicly—that's important, as we noted in the introduction.

What product(s) will students create?

We use the term "product" but that doesn't always mean it's a tangible object. It's anything students *produce*; it could be an event, a service, a presentation, or a performance. There are many, many different types of products, and a key question to ask yourself for a particular project is, is the product authentic? Is it what people in the world outside of school would create in this situation? Does it serve a real purpose? Is it intended for a specific audience or end-user?

Here are some examples of different types of products:

Written products:

Research report
Letter
Brochure
Script
Book review
Training manual
Mathematical/engineering
    analysis
Blog
Scientific study/experiment
Video/animation
Content for website
Computer program/app
Digital story/comic
Editorial

Media and technology products:

Audio recording/podcast
Slideshow
Drawing/painting

Collage/scrapbook
Photo essay
Video/animation
Storyboard
Website
Computer program/app
Digital story/comic
Social media campaign

Constructed products:

Small-scale model
Consumer product
Device/machine
Vehicle
Invention
Scientific instrument
Museum exhibit
Structure
Garden

Presentations:

Speech
Debate
Oral presentation/defense
Newscast
Panel discussion
Play/dramatic presentation
Poetry slam/storytelling
Musical piece or dance
Lesson
Public event
Sales pitch

Planning products:

Proposal
Business plan
Design
Bid or estimate
Blueprint
Timeline
Flow chart

In addition to the question of authenticity, here are some more considerations when choosing products for a project:

Does the product provide enough evidence that students have met the targeted learning goals, or is a combination of products needed?

In some projects, the product might be enough. For example, a written research report in science or social studies, sent to an organization, could contain the content knowledge and demonstrate the thinking and writing skills targeted. In other projects, if students are creating models of a container they've designed, you might need a written artifact as well, to explain the mathematics used. (See more about choosing the right products in Chapter 2, "Aligning Projects to Standards.")

Is the product feasible?

Think about whether you and your students can create the product, given constraints such as time, expertise, cost of materials or equipment, and the students' age and experience. You may need to scale back your and your students' ambitions. Instead of actually building a tiny house, for example, maybe a blueprint or scale model will do. Or instead of a full-length play, have students write and perform scenes.

What products will be created by individual students or done as a team?

This is a common concern in PBL, raising issues of accountability and assessment (including "group grades" which we suggest minimizing the use of—see Chapter 5, "Assessing Student Learning"). For example, a team presentation might not allow you to assess individual students, so you'd also need to require an individually written piece.

Will students be able to choose what product they create, or will they all create the same product?

Allowing students to choose the product they will create is a common and important way to include the Essential Element "Student Voice & Choice" in a project. It increases buy-in, honors their wisdom, and allows them to express their unique voice. You should coach students when they choose products, to help make sure they're good choices. Or, depending on the needs and PBL experience level of your students, you may want to provide a list of products to choose from, so you can make sure they're feasible and appropriate. Be aware, too, that having multiple products in a project makes it more complicated for you to manage and assess.

The nature of the project may dictate what products students create. For example, if it's a "local history museum" project, each team would need to create an exhibit, although the design of their exhibits could vary. Or if it's a whole-class project, say, to create a website to publish student-written fan fiction, teams might tackle various aspects of the task, but they're all focused on one final product. In other projects, multiple products might be required to fully answer a driving question or address a problem. See the matrix below for the options.

Options for Product Creation

Same product, same focus	Different product, same focus
Example: Each team makes a presentation of their solution to a community problem.	*Example:* Teams create posters, PSA videos, or a social media campaign to address the same issue in the community.
Same product, different focus	Different product, different focus
Example: Each team creates a social media campaign to raise awareness about a community issue of their choice.	*Example:* Teams create posters, PSA videos, or a social media campaign to raise awareness about a community issue of their choice.

How will students make their work public?
This brings up another common stereotype about PBL: that every project has to culminate with a grand exhibition or presentation to an audience. Although that may be the best way to end a project, think more broadly about what "make work public" means—and when it happens during a project. It can be *during* a project too, when students are drafting their ideas or creating plans and prototypes for products, and are seeking feedback from experts or potential users or audiences. Students can also make their work public during a project by showing it in draft form to peers for critique and revision, as well as sharing a final product. The point is, students are not just handing in their work to a teacher.

Making Work Public Online

Below are just a few of our current favorite tech tools students can use to share work with people beyond the classroom. Remember to include a way to collect feedback, so people can ask questions, offer comments, or assess the work.

Padlet: For creating discussions, capturing need to knows, or helping students to visually organize their thoughts and learning.

Adobe Spark: Provides templates for short videos, graphic design projects, or visually striking websites.

Bookcreator: Excellent publication tool with intuitive design that makes it a great tool for students of all ages and abilities.

Soundtrap: Collaborative audio tool that allows students to create and produce musical projects online.

Explain Everything: Video production and sharing tool to create screencasts, record presentations, or make simple animations.

You can find many more resources and tech tools for creating and sharing student work online at *commonsensemedia.org*.

Here are some examples of possible public audiences for projects:

- Panel of stakeholders (real or fictitious)
- Experts
- Users of a product
- People from local government, businesses, civic and nonprofit organizations
- Audience for a piece of writing, media, art, or a performance, at events or on the web
- Audience for a social media campaign
- Students of other ages or in other places
- Family and friends
- School staff members

Make the process public, not just the product

One more key point, when planning how students will make their work public: allow time and structure it so students can, as the Project Design Rubric states, "explain the reasoning behind choices they made, their inquiry process, how they worked, what they learned, etc." Again, this should happen both during a project when students are developing their answer to a driving question and their products, and at the end when they share completed work.

Having students explain their thinking and the process of completing the project is important for several reasons. It teaches students to be reflective and metacognitive, which is a valuable critical thinking skill. It helps with retention, as thinking and talking or writing explicitly about the process one follows to complete a task helps cement it into memory and transfer it to other tasks in the future (Mergendoller, 2017).

Having students explain their thinking and process also serves as a demonstration of learning, providing opportunities for assessment, both formative and summative. For example, if a student shares their problem-solving process mid-way through a project, flaws can be spotted and corrected. At the end of a project, students can be asked to reflect on and document their use of critical thinking, problem-solving, creativity, collaboration, and other success skills. Publicly discussing the use of these skills, as evidenced in student work and their reflections, also gives teachers and school leaders helpful guidance on how to better develop and report on students' attainment of the skills.

See Chapter 4, "Managing Activities," for more details on how to manage presentations and other ways students can make their work public.

Determining a Time Frame

Projects can vary greatly in length, and there are several factors to consider. It depends on the topic and subject area, the nature of the project and its major products, and your and your students' choices. There also may be external constraints like pacing guides and the school calendar with its schedule of events, including test-taking and assessment. Having an outside organization involved in a project might also dictate the time frame for a project, if, say, they need a product done by a certain date or can only work with students for a specific time.

At a minimum, a project needs to be long enough to contain all seven Essential Project Design Elements—which means time for investigation, gaining knowledge and skills, creation of a product or answer to a driving question, and making work public. Some elements could be developed to a lesser extent in a short project; for example, you might not have a formal presentation, and the inquiry process would not be in-depth, over time.

	Typical Length	Examples	Notes
Short Project	3–5 days/5–8 hours of class time	• mini-projects to start the year and introduce PBL to students, build culture • projects focused on 1-2 standards, simple products • single-subject projects	• can be in all subject areas; often seen in math, career/tech, and world languages
Average Project	3-5 weeks/12-25 hours of class time	• includes most teacher-guided projects • can be multi-subject area	• most of the work is done in class, or in remote learning with close monitoring/coaching by teacher
Long Project	6 weeks or more/ 25+ hours of class time	• includes ambitious projects focused on big ideas, complex problems, multiple products • often seen for senior projects and other independently done projects on topics chosen by students	• not every day in class is necessarily spent on project work • independently done projects are mostly completed outside of class time

Here are some things to consider when planning your project's time frame:

- Given that the teacher needs to monitor and coach students throughout a project, how much should and can they get done outside of scheduled class time?
- Can students engage with content independently via online/video resources and then apply it during synchronous or in-person learning time?
- How many standards or other learning goals are being targeted, and how much time would it take to learn and practice them? If there aren't too many and they're not too complex, a short project may do.

Identifying milestones

Like a journey, a project has a beginning, middle, and end. Here is the typical path most projects take, which we've separated into four phases. These phases are similar to those found in models for design thinking and engineering.

Project Path

PHASE 1
Launch Project: Entry Event and Driving Question

PHASE 2
Build Knowledge, Understanding and Skills to Answer Driving Question

PHASE 3
Develop and Critique Products and Answers to Driving Question

PHASE 4
Present Products and Answers to the Driving Question

REVISION

In each phase of the project path there are "milestones": key events or tasks in a project that mark its progress, from Day One to its completion. Typical milestones are the entry event that launches a project, checkpoints for tasks such as completing research notes and rough drafts/plans/prototypes, deadlines for completed products, and presentations (or however students are making their work public). Most milestones have at least one formative assessment that informs the decision about whether and when to move on to the next milestone.

On the next page are the milestones in a sample project from the PBLWorks project library, where you can find more details—plus many more examples from various subject areas and grade levels.

Creating a project calendar

The last major step in designing and planning a project is to map out what's going to happen day-by-day. How much detail you want to include is up to you. It depends on the nature of the project, your personal preference, your students, and the degree of choice they're going to have.

The milestones you've planned can go on the calendar first, from the launch day to the culminating events or activities. Be sure to build in plenty of time for critique and revision, and for reflection both during and at the end of the project.

As you're planning the day-to-day, remember what we said in the introduction. You can leverage a lot of the teaching strategies, lessons, activities, formative assessments, etc. that you used to teach content and skills before you became a PBL teacher, but now they're contextualized within the project.

Changing the World One Poem at a Time

Driving Question:	**How can we use poetry to promote social justice in our community?**
Project Summary:	Each student chooses a social justice poem, finds or creates accompanying images that enhance the poem's meaning, and record an expressive oral performance of the poem. Teams collaborate to produce a montage video that ties their poems together around a common theme. Students also create a response poem or social justice poem of their own, inspired by one of their classmates' selected poems. Finally, students work together as a class to create a community exhibition featuring their video montages as well as their original poems paired with images and the mentor texts that inspired them.
MILESTONE 1: Entry event	Students visit a local library, peace and justice center, literary or nonprofit organization, or learn from a guest speaker; then they are asked to create an exhibition of poetry. Students learn more about the project and generate a list of need to know questions. Formative assessment is a written "exit ticket" about how students are reflecting on social justice issues at this point.
MILESTONE 2: Poem analysis (individual)	Students identify a social justice issue they care about; then they find and analyze a poem about it. Formative assessment is a written analysis.
MILESTONE 3: Poem performance (individual)	Students expressively perform their poems and show visual images they have curated or created to go with it. Their performances are formatively assessed in a peer critique protocol.
MILESTONE 4: Video recording with visuals (team)	In teams, students decide on a theme that connects their poems and create a video montage with a recording of them performing their poems. A storyboard is used for formative assessment.
MILESTONE 5: Original poem (individual)	Students write a response poem or a social justice poem of their own inspired by one of the mentor texts, which are formatively assessed in a peer critique protocol.
MILESTONE 6: Public exhibition (team)	Students share their video montages in a public exhibition.

Keep in mind that the project may shift if students become really interested in something, or the circumstances require giving it more time—so your calendar needs to be flexible to some extent. Certain days may have to be set, such as if and when external experts or organizations are going to be working with students, when field work is happening, or when a culminating event needs to take place. But in between those days, build in some flexible time for more learning if needed, and for both individual and team work.

Some Final Tips & Ideas

> Create student handouts before launching a project, such as a project information sheet, research note-taking forms, team contract templates—plus, if you want to be really prepared, other documents you will need for various lessons.

> Create rubrics in advance, although these may be co-created with students during the project. (See more on rubrics in Chapter 5, "Assessing Student Learning.")

> Arrange in advance any resources you'll need for the project. This could mean people—from content experts to community members to school staff—or it could be materials, equipment, or facilities on campus or in the community.

> Two of the most important ideas in this chapter are "know your students" and "authenticity."

> Planning a Gold Standard PBL project might seem daunting if you're new to it, so to reassure you, remember (a) it gets easier when you gain experience, and (b) you'll feel more relaxed during the project compared to how it might feel to prep for traditional instruction every day.

✱ NOTES ✱

Project Based Learning Handbook

CHAPTER 2

Aligning to Standards

L ET'S BEGIN THIS CHAPTER WITH A STORY FROM a teacher who learned a lesson about the importance of aligning projects to rigorous learning goals.

> *In the spring of my second year in the classroom, I experienced my first project exhibition. Exhibitions at this school, which emphasized PBL, were elaborate affairs where students presented their work to extended families and community members, answering questions, persuading audiences, and demonstrating not only their mastery of content but also their polished presentation skills and high-quality finished projects.*

My students' exhibition would be the final product of a lengthy world history unit on the Holocaust and modern genocides. Students had learned extensively about the history of Europe leading up to the Holocaust, Hitler's rise to power, the effects of fascism, and harrowing experiences in the concentration camps. They had chosen another, more recent genocide to study, and had impressively become experts on the genocides in Rwanda, Darfur, Guatemala, and Cambodia.

The final products in the unit were genocide memorials, created collaboratively in teams, that would make up a "Genocide Memorial Museum" for our guests. Power tools were employed, barbed wire affixed to various structures, and earnest attempts were made to portray xenophobia, suffering, and genocide through art.

The night arrived and students placed their memorials throughout the school, ready to answer audience questions and hopeful of winning awards. It wasn't until I could see all of their work on display that I realized something had gone terribly wrong.

You could look at each memorial and have absolutely no idea what they were memorializing. I hadn't asked students to create plaques detailing the genocide they had learned about. None of the questions in the parent program asked about the causes of genocide, elicited comparisons between the Holocaust and this genocide, or prompted students to explain the long-lasting effects the genocide had on the survivors. In short, aside from their proficiency with power tools and glue guns, their final products did little to demonstrate any student learning.

Since that exhibition, years ago, I keep that project in my head every time I start planning a new project. It taught me many things about what not to do when designing high-quality PBL but, most importantly, it showed me the importance of tying a project to rigorous and important standards. **"**

The "Genocide Memorial Museum" project described above could be improved in several ways. For one thing, it has some features of "dessert" projects rather than "main course" PBL, because creating the museum exhibit was not the focus of the unit. The unit's content knowledge and academic concepts were taught first, *then* the students built their memorials. The memorials were more of a demonstration and expression of what students had learned, rather than being the driver of the unit. But most important, as the teacher ruefully noted, the memorial exhibition did not include enough evidence of learning; it was not aligned with important content standards.

To many people, including teachers who are new to it, the term "Project Based Learning" brings up images of impressive-looking products students have created. Opportunities to create "beautiful work," in Ron Berger's words, are certainly valuable for students. However, if those opportunities aren't thoughtfully paired with rigorous, high-level standards that allow our students to gain important knowledge, deepen understanding of concepts, and develop key success skills, we are doing them a disservice. That's why we put student learning goals in the center of our model for Gold Standard PBL and made "Align to Standards" one of the seven Project Based Teaching Practices.

"Align to Standards" in the Project Based Teaching Rubric:

> Criteria for products are clearly and specifically derived from standards and allow demonstration of mastery.

> Scaffolding of student learning, critique and revision protocols, assessments, and rubrics consistently refer to and support student achievement of specific standards.

Starting from Standards when Designing a Project

In Chapter 1, we talked about how, when designing and planning a project, you might start with an idea or start with standards. Let's flesh out how the latter approach works. The basic process is to identify the content standards you want students to learn, then think of a project in which students could demonstrate that they have done so.

First, let's clarify what we mean by "standards." Standards encompass all of the things you consider essential for students to learn in order to be successful in your class. That includes the content-area standards your school, district, or state has mandated for your course, but think outside the box—it can also include:

- Cross-curricular competencies your school may have set, such as research/inquiry, creative expression, and analysis
- Success skills: critical thinking, collaboration, communication, creativity, project management, etc.
- School or district "graduate profiles" or school-wide outcomes
- Grade-level or disciplinary literacy goals
- Characteristics of life-long learners such as growth mindset, self-advocacy, curiosity
- Humanizing qualities: empathy, selflessness, activism, global mindset

Narrowing Down Your Standards

Depending on how specifically your standards or curriculum guide documents are written, don't try to pack too many into one project. Here's a good test: think about how long it would take you to teach particular standards in a traditional curriculum unit. Since a "main course" project is equivalent to a unit, that's about as many standards you should target.

To help narrow down the standards to focus on for a project, ask yourself the following questions:

- Does this standard take significant time and practice to master, or do I usually cover it in a few days?
- Which standards are complex, requiring demonstration and real-world application, not just simple memorization or recall?
- Is it vital that students have mastered the standard before they move on to the next unit of study?
- Is there something happening in the community or broader world right now that would make the practice of a particular standard more relevant and authentic?
- What standards make sense to teach at this time of year?

Also, think about whether some standards can be in the *foreground*—those you explicitly teach and assess in the project—while others can be in the *background*—skills that are required and practiced but not explicitly taught and assessed? For example, informational writing might be a skill used in a project that students have previously learned, so it's in the background; standards for new content knowledge would be in the foreground.

PBL PRO TIP

Share Standards with Students

Be clear with students about which standards they might be practicing and which you are explicitly teaching and assessing during the project. The more we can pull back that curtain and show students the thinking behind our project design, the more they can take ownership of their progress toward mastery of the standards.

"Marie Kondo" Your Curriculum

The Covid-19 pandemic caused many educators to reconsider what students really need to learn in school. Fears of students "falling behind" led to plans to double-down on "covering" the curriculum by increasing the number of instructional days, requiring summer school, and having teachers simply cram more standards into already-crowded courses.

Instead, we should be narrowing down the curriculum to what is really essential, according to researcher Jal Mehta and teacher Shanna Peeples in their article, "Marie Kondo the Curriculum" (Albert Shanker Institute, June 25, 2020). They suggest identifying these five types of learning goals, which have implications for PBL:

1. Topics that spiral, such as essay-writing, which repeat over the years, so students do not need to "catch up". (These can be revisited in many projects from K–12.)

2. Topics that are nice to haves, but not vital, so let them go. (Don't overstuff projects with them.)

3. Topics that are sequential, where students really do need to learn something before they can learn something else. These are found in math, especially. But be judicious and limit it to things that are really needed before you can teach what's next. (Think in terms of "just in time" learning; what will students need to know in order to do a particular project?)

4. Topics that really are essential, in order to be an educated person and citizen. (These are good choices for projects.)

5. Skills, like reading and writing, that benefit from practice and repeated exposure. The authors note, "It is important that kids practice these things, but there is no reason why they need to become decontextualized from the reasons why you might want to do them." (This connects to how PBL gives students an authentic "need to know" content and skills.)

Aligning Products to Standards

Once you've selected the right standards to guide your project, it's time to align the project's major products with them. We discussed the range of possible products in Chapter 1; here we'll focus on making sure they will provide adequate evidence that students have met the standards.

First, think deeply about authenticity. Here are some questions you might ask yourself—and your students, if you are co-designing a project—when deciding what products to create:

- Where do these standards appear in the world outside of school?
- What kinds of professionals do the type of thinking required by these standards?
- What is happening today in our community, or in the broader world, that could connect to these standards?
- Where do my students see themselves in the standards? Do they have personal interests or backgrounds that could lead to meaningful personal connections?

This is the key question for aligning products with standards: What product(s) will allow you to meaningfully assess student mastery of each standard? Note that it usually will need to be a combination of products, because it's often impossible to assess all the standards in one single product, or to assess individual student learning in a team-created product. And some standards may need to be assessed via "smaller" assignments or checks—for example, a quiz or a short piece of writing that is not considered a "product" per se.

The following two tables, one for middle school and one for high school, show how sample projects from the pblworks.org project library allow for meaningful demonstration of key standards in the final product.

Aligned Standards & Products: Middle School

Standard(s)	Products	Evidence of Meaningful Alignment
CCSS Middle School Mathematics 6.RP.A.1 Understand the concept of a ratio and use ratio language to describe a ratio relationship between two quantities. 6.RP.A.2 Understand the concept of a unit rate a/b associated with a ratio a:b with b not equal to zero, and use rate language in the context of a ratio relationship. 6.RP.A.3.C Find a percent of a quantity as a rate per 100 (e.g., 30% of a quantity means 30/100 times the quantity); solve problems involving finding the whole, given a part and the percent.	**Project: *Quadrats to Biodiversity*** Students conduct a quadrat survey by marking out rectangular frames in a sample area in order to investigate the health of a local ecosystem such as their school grounds or a nearby park. They use the data collected to calculate the abundance of different species as both a measure of density (unit rate) and of frequency (percentage). They analyze the health of the ecosystem (using ratios and percentages), either by focusing on an invasive species or by examining the biodiversity of the ecosystem. Students present their findings and discuss their implications in the form of a news article.	Students create data tables showing calculations of the density and frequency of data collected. Teams write news articles about their survey results, explaining how results were calculated and what they mean.
Next Generation Science Standards MS-ETS1-1 Define the criteria and constraints of a design problem with sufficient precision to ensure a successful solution, taking into account relevant scientific principles and potential impacts on people and the natural environment that may limit possible solutions.* MS-ESS3-3 Apply scientific principles to design a method for monitoring and minimizing a human impact on the environment.* *(*partially addressed)*	**Project: *Making Space for Change*** Students are charged with the task of creating an environmentally sustainable redesign for a community space, such as a park, library, public square, empty lot, or community center. Students visit the space; research the local context, needs, resources, and constraints; and investigate principles of environmentally sustainable design. Student teams engage in critique and revision processes that involve local community members and then present their solutions to key stakeholders.	Students individually create written and/or illustrated components of their prototype design of the community space, including all aspects of the standards targeted. Teams explain their product and the process used to develop it in terms of the standards.

Standard(s)	Products	Evidence of Meaningful Alignment
C3 Framework for Social Studies D2.His.1.6-8 Analyze connections among events and developments in broader historical contexts. D2.His.2.6-8 Classify series of historical events and developments as examples of change and/or continuity. D2.His.3.6-8 Use questions generated about individuals and groups to analyze why they, and the developments they shaped, are seen as historically significant. D2.His.14.6-8 Explain multiple causes and effects of events and developments in the past. D2.His.15.6-8 Evaluate the relative influence of various causes of events and developments in the past. D2.His.16.6-8 Organize applicable evidence into a coherent argument about the past. **CCSS Literacy in History/ Social Studies, Science, & Technical Subjects** W.6-8.1 Write arguments focused on discipline-specific content. W.6-8.1.B Support claim(s) with logical reasoning and relevant, accurate data and evidence that demonstrate an understanding of the topic or text, using credible sources.	**Project:** *Golden Age* Working in teams, students choose a particular civilization and conduct research on its "golden age" and why it declined or ended, then they communicate what they learned through a museum exhibit. The exhibits are displayed at a community/school event to which other students, parents, and community members are invited. Students are prepared to summarize their conclusions when asked by visitors to their museum exhibit. Individually, students collect research notes and write an argument for what lessons we can learn from history that can be applied to our own civilization in the present day. They publish these arguments in a booklet that serves as a companion guide to the museum exhibit.	Each student collects and submits a set of research notes that correspond to the history standards targeted. Each student uses their notes to create a piece of argumentative writing about lessons learned from history that can be applied to contemporary society.

Aligned Standards & Products: High School

Standard(s)	Products	Evidence of Meaningful Alignment
CCSS High School ELA: Reading: Literature RL.9-10.1: Cite strong and thorough textual evidence to support analysis of what the text says explicitly as well as inferences drawn from the text. RL.9-10.2: Determine a theme or central idea of a text and analyze in detail its development over the course of the text, including how it emerges and is shaped and refined by specific details; provide an objective summary of the text.	**Project: *Literary Playlist*** Students read and analyze a piece of literature, and then publish their playlists, along with a detailed set of "liner notes" that provide an evidence-based analysis of the themes or character development throughout the written work and a rationale for the selection of each song. Students share their playlists and liner notes via social media and/or on a class website.	The playlist asks students to identify themes in the texts and select songs that show their analysis of those themes. Liner notes require students to cite strong textual evidence connecting their playlists to the themes they have drawn from the text.
CCSS High School Mathematics HSS.ID.B.6: Represent data on two quantitative variables on a scatter plot, and describe how variables are related. HSF.IF.B.4: For a function that models a relationship between two quantities, interpret key features of graphs and tables in terms of the quantities, and sketch graphs showing key features given a verbal description of the relationship. HSF.BF.A.1: Write a function that describes a relationship between two quantities.	**Project: *Parabolas for Profit*** In this project, students take on the role of market research analysts working for locally owned companies. Students analyze the linear relationships between cost and quantity of items sold, along with the quadratic relationships of total profit and unit price, to determine the most profitable price point for one of the goods or services the company sells. Students create a written market research analysis report, and they present their findings to business owners.	A market analysis report and presentation to business owners asks students to show the most profitable price point for products or services and support that claim with data representations (scatter plots, graphs, and tables) while also explaining the mathematical thinking in writing and in a spoken explanation.

Standard(s)	Products	Evidence of Meaningful Alignment
Next Generation Science Standards HS-PS2-1: Analyze data to support the claim that Newton's second law of motion describes the mathematical relationship among the net force on a macroscopic object, its mass, and its acceleration. HS-PS2-3: Apply scientific and engineering ideas to design, evaluate, and refine a device that minimizes the force on a macroscopic object during a collision. HS-ETS1-3: Evaluate a solution to a complex real-world problem based on prioritized criteria and trade-offs that account for a range of constraints, including cost, safety, reliability, and aesthetics as well as possible social, cultural, and environmental impacts.	**Project: *Crash Course!*** In this project, students identify situations in which individuals need protection from collisions or impact and then propose and build protective solutions. Some examples might include more secure baby strollers or shopping carts, helmets for high-impact sports such as skateboarding, football, or biking, or a shoe design that lowers the impact of running. Students write up a design brief for a manufacturer, to include an analysis of the problem (and pertinent calculations) along with a design for a proposed solution.	The design brief asks students to analyze data that shows the problem, with relevant calculations from Newton's second law of motion, and then use scientific and engineering ideas to create solutions to that problem. By conferring with and presenting to experts in the field, such as manufacturers, designers, and engineers, students must situate their solution in a real-world context and account for constraints accordingly.

Centering Standards Throughout the Project

As you plan a project, certainly a lot of the work of aligning it to standards happens in the initial planning and designing process. However, if we're truly going to ensure that students are learning deeply throughout the project, it is vital to continue to center the standards throughout its implementation.

You can do this through the use of student questions, formative assessment, and reflection.

Student Questions

As we explained in the introduction, student questions are central to sustained inquiry in PBL. The process of generating questions begins at the launch, and continues during the project—and you should connect the questions with the standards.

As we said in Chapter 1, you don't need to use the exact language of standards in the project's driving question. However, when students identify what they already know about the topic and what they need to know in order to answer the driving question, you can coach them to ask questions that connect to standards. For example, if the driving question is, How can we design a park that children in our community will safely enjoy? student questions might include:

- What do the kids and families in our community want in a park?
- What do engineers consider when they are designing parks?
- How many children in our community are likely to play in the park at any given time of day? How big does the park need to be? How many swings do we need?
- What kinds of cushioning materials will keep children from getting hurt if they fall, from what height?
- What is a safe but fun angle and height for a slide? Do toddlers and older kids need different kinds of slides?
- How do we calculate the materials, construction, and maintenance costs for different park options? What can our community afford to build and maintain?

Once students have developed questions that will drive their inquiry throughout the project, you can spend some time together, or on your own, matching those questions to standards. Ask yourself, What standard will students need to meet to answer this question? Organizing these key student questions by standards can also help you identify gaps in your planning.

Formative Assessment

The use of formative assessment, as we explain in Chapter 5, "Assessing Student Learning," is a prominent feature of PBL. It will help you gauge how effectively your students are moving toward mastery of the standards throughout the project. It can start from Day One when you analyze students' need to know questions, allowing you to identify what they already know and what's missing from their prior knowledge.

All throughout the project, keep the standards at the forefront of your formative assessment strategies. For example:

- Include language from standards in rubrics or other sets of quality criteria you and your students develop.
- When students use the rubrics or criteria in critique protocols or other formative assessment opportunities, have them refer explicitly to standards.
- Make sure other formative assessments, such as quizzes, checks for understanding, or feedback on rough drafts and prototypes link directly to standards.

Reflection

Use reflection as a tool to help students internalize the standards and allow them to truly take ownership of their learning. As noted above, the more students are actively engaged in the process of identifying their need to know questions in relation to the standards, creating quality criteria and regularly checking their progress toward mastery, the more they'll be able to authentically reflect on their work throughout the project.

Some possible student reflection questions to consider:

- What will a finished product look like if it demonstrates these standards?
- Where am I right now? What parts of this project sound do-able, and where am I more likely to need help or extra effort?
- What jobs that I know of ask people to practice these skills or use this knowledge?
- If we're focused on these standards, what will I need to learn to be able to complete this project?
- In my team, who is going to be able to help me get better at this skill?
- Who needs help in my team with something that I am already good at?
- How can I revise my work to show mastery?
- How did I get better at this skill in the last few weeks?
- For a skill I haven't improved in, what is my roadblock? Do I need more practice or more help?

Here's another idea for an ongoing routine that students can use to reflect on the learning goals for a project, from Oakland International High School and Stanford Center for Assessment, Learning, & Equity (SCALE).

Ask students to put specific standards or other learning goals in one of these three "zones":

1. Their "comfort zone"—what is easy for you to learn?
2. Their "stretch zone"—what is something you can learn with some effort?
3. Their "struggle zone"—what is something that is really challenging for you to learn?

For each zone, students can reflect, alone or in teams, on why they put the goal where they did, what activities have been helpful in learning it, and what next steps they could take to learn it better if need be.

Some Final Tips & Ideas

Standards won't fully live in your projects unless you consistently use them and explicitly refer to them throughout the project. Here are some ways both students and teachers can keep them front and center:

Teachers can:

❯ Post standards, in student-friendly language as appropriate, on the classroom (or digital) wall along with exemplars of work aligned with those standards.

❯ Create a graphic showing the final product(s) and noting how/where the standards will show up.

❯ Daily, identify and explicitly name which standards students are working on as they move through the phases of a project.

❯ Create and maintain a public, class-wide progress chart showing average progress toward mastery of the standards being used in the project. (This can be used to create healthy competition between classes as well!).

❯ Create a spreadsheet for yourself, tracking how many times each student has practiced the standard and where they currently are in terms of mastery.

Students can:

❯ Co-craft quality criteria with teachers, to ensure they understand what high-quality work will look like in terms of the standards.

❯ Maintain a tracker for themselves, noting their progress toward mastery of each standard and updating as they improve.

❯ Set goals for reaching standards between formative assessments.

✳ NOTES ✳

CHAPTER 3

Building the Culture

THE CULTURE OF A CLASSROOM WHERE STUDENTS are experiencing Project Based Learning is different from the culture typically seen in a classroom with traditional instruction. Although there are times during a project when students may be sitting quietly listening to the teacher, at other times you would see, hear, and sense the difference.

Students will be active. It can get noisy, but more often it's a "productive hum." We've described a PBL classroom as being like a healthy, high-functioning modern workplace. You'd see tables and perhaps special work areas, not just rows of individual desks. You might see students working in teams, using tech tools, or practicing a presentation. You would hear students' voices. You would sense inclusivity, mutual respect, and shared ownership.

In short, it's a learning community.

Culture is defined as "the set of shared attitudes, values, goals, and practices that characterizes an institution or organization." It's not built in a day or a week, but in

"Build the Culture" in the Project Based Teaching Rubric:

▸ Norms to guide the classroom are co-crafted with and self-monitored by students.

▸ Student voice and choice is regularly leveraged and ongoing, including identification of real-world issues and problems students want to address in projects.

▸ Students usually know what they need to do with minimal direction from the teacher.

▸ Students work collaboratively in healthy, high-functioning teams, much like an authentic work environment; the teacher rarely needs to be involved in managing teams.

▸ Students understand there is no single "right answer" or preferred way to do the project and that it is OK to take risks, make mistakes, and learn from them.

▸ The values of critique and revision, persistence, rigorous thinking and pride in doing high-quality work are shared and students hold one another accountable to them.

a constant, ongoing process. We touch upon aspects of culture in several chapters in this book—it's reflected in the way you design a project, engage and coach, assess, scaffold, and manage. In this chapter we'll focus on some additional strategies for building and maintaining it.

PBL PRO TIP

Be a Thermostat, Not a Thermometer

Jason Barger, author of the book *Thermostat Cultures*, offers this advice for managers and leaders of teams, which applies to the active role of the teacher in building a culture for PBL:

"A thermometer just reads the temperature in a room. It is reactionary and all it does is tell you the temperature. A thermostat sets the temperature, regulates the temperature, controls the temperature. Thermostats proactively initiate positive change into the culture."

Why is culture important?

A healthy classroom culture makes students and teachers feel better about being there, and it helps with classroom and project management. But it goes beyond warm feelings, comfort and ease; the right culture improves learning and promotes equity.

Education research provides substantial evidence for the beneficial effects of school and classroom culture on learning. This is especially true for students from historically underserved groups. Here's a sampling of what you can find in the literature:

> *"Classroom environment is one of the most important factors affecting student learning. Simply put, students learn better when they view the learning environment as positive and supportive (Dorman, Aldridge, & Fraser, 2006). A positive environment is one in which students feel a sense of belonging, trust others, and feel encouraged to tackle challenges, take risks, and ask questions (Bucholz & Sheffler, 2009)."*
>
> – **Joan Young**, *Encouragement in the Classroom* (ASCD 2014)

"Students who are confident they belong and are valued by their teachers and peers are able to engage more fully in learning. They have fewer behavior problems, are more open to critical feedback, take greater advantage of learning opportunities, build important relationships, and generally have more positive attitudes about their classwork and teachers. In turn, they are more likely to persevere in the face of difficulty and do better in school."

— **Carissa Romero**, "What We Know About Belonging from Scientific Research" (2015, Mindset Scholar's Network, Stanford University)

> **FOR REMOTE LEARNING** — **PBL Culture = What Works Best**

Project Based Learning was reported to be effective in remote learning environments in 2020, as we discussed in the introduction of this book. The culture that sustains PBL is a big reason why.

Prominent education researcher Linda Darling-Hammond said this in her 2020 report, *Restarting and Reinventing School*:

"A group of more than 400 researchers offering advice about education during this time (the Covid-19 pandemic) urged that schools 'provide the most personalized and engaging instruction possible'. Learning opportunities are most effective when they start with meaningful questions; provide opportunities for inquiry in interaction with others; enable hands-on experiences and applications to meaningful contexts; and provide frequent, informative feedback on what students are doing and thinking in identity-safe environments."

If you're teaching in a remote or blended learning setting, what are the implications of this quote on your own experience?

*"The belief that one is academically and socially connected, supported, and respected...
is one of three learning mindsets—along with growth mindset and a sense of purpose
and relevance—that help us understand the deeper structure of motivation. A sense
of belonging helps shape students' beliefs about themselves, their potential, and the
learning context, and is likely to be especially beneficial for students from traditionally marginalized groups."*

– **Ian Kelleher**, "Using High Expectations to Boost Students' Sense of Belonging"
(Edutopia, Dec. 2020)

Relationships and Power Dynamics

Let's begin the how-to of building a PBL culture by talking about two ideas that
are fundamental to it: relationships—between the teacher and students and among
students—and power.

Relationships between teachers and students are closer in PBL than what you typically
find in traditional instruction, especially in secondary schools. And the basis of a close
relationship is knowing each other well. As we've said in other chapters in this book,
knowing your students is key to PBL. It's important for designing meaningful projects,
managing activities, and engaging and coaching students. It's also vital when building
the classroom culture.

Learning about your students' strengths, interests, and needs makes them feel known.
It sends a powerful message that they are valued as individuals and as members of
the classroom community. It's about honoring the wisdom and ways of knowing that
your students bring into the classroom, too. We want students to understand that they
already know many things and can easily build upon and apply that knowledge into
their work on projects.

Here are some ways to build relationships with students—many of which apply to
good teaching generally, but are especially important for PBL:

- Greet students at the classroom door.
- Learn about students' interests, needs, talents, and preferences.
- Communicate with families or other teachers for a broader understanding of
  students' capabilities.
- Eat lunch with small groups of students.

- Have 1:1 and small group conferences with students.
- Meet with focus groups of students.
- Ask students for feedback on learning activities.
- Communicate with families through a newsletter or blog.
- Call home to communicate student accomplishments.
- Attend student sporting events or other extracurricular activities.
- Within appropriate boundaries, share details about yourself, such as interests, hobbies, strengths, and struggles.

Reducing the Number of Student Contacts to Know Them Better

Getting to know your students is challenging when you teach 150 of them, which is often the case in many secondary schools. It will take longer than it does in elementary schools, for sure, but it is possible—and while each student is unique, many of them will have common characteristics.

Middle schools tend to be smaller than high schools, which makes it easier to know students, and many have instituted structural changes such as block schedules and team teaching that reduce the total number of student contacts.

At the high school level, career academies, special programs, and schools-within-schools have been found to be effective in enabling teachers to better know their students. And most alternative, independent, and charter schools are smaller than regular public high schools in urban and suburban areas. Consider an advisory program, in which teachers stay with a small cohort of students over time, or "looping" in which a single graded class stays with a teacher for two or more years.

Relationships between students

PBL also deepens and transforms relationships between students. In PBL classrooms, students frequently work in collaborative teams and hold one another accountable to shared agreements. They help each other improve and learn by using feedback protocols. Rather than viewing academic achievement as a form of competition, students develop a sense of interdependence and collective responsibility for one another's learning and success. (For more on building healthy student teams, see Chapter 4, "Managing Activities." For more on feedback protocols, see Chapter 5, "Assessing Student Learning.")

To build this collaborative, supportive culture, students need to get to know each other too—or know each other differently—so consider strategies such as:

- Do "get-to-know-you" activities at the beginning of the year or semester.
- Offer opportunities for students to collaborate on interest-based mini-projects or assignments.
- Use varied structures (such as Think-Pair-Share or Inside-Outside circles) to support student-student interactions and conversations.
- Start the class with a check-in question or prompt, inviting students to share their perspectives or experiences related to a topic with partners, small groups, or the whole class.
- Change seating arrangement regularly.
- Create a digital classroom discussion forum in which students respond to prompts about culture or content related topics.
- Incorporate restorative circles and other practices that help students learn about one another and address power dynamics in the classroom.

A power shift

Since relationships in a PBL environment are more collaborative, that means power is shared more than it is in a traditional "top-down" classroom. PBL challenges typical notions of power in education by giving students voice and choice. We ask them to help identify issues and problems they find meaningful to address in projects, to co-create norms and agreements, and to work collaboratively with their peers to solve problems.

The coaching role of the PBL teacher also shifts the power dynamic. Students see the teacher less as an authority figure or disciplinarian and more as someone who's "on their side," helping them meet the challenge of the project. PBL teachers are also focused on authenticity—not only when designing projects, but when they build upon knowledge of students and students' communities to create the classroom culture.

Building Culture Through Shared Beliefs and Values

Here are some of the beliefs and values that build and sustain a PBL culture:

- We show mutual respect, cultural responsiveness, and an appreciation for diverse learning styles, orientations, backgrounds, and experiences.
- We have high expectations and a growth mindset—every student, with the right learning scaffolds and differentiation structures, can and will achieve and succeed.
- We take pride in doing high-quality work, and that's why we value critique and revision, persistence, and rigorous thinking.
- We value inquiry and questioning, and understand that a project's driving question is open-ended—there is no single "right answer" or preferred way to do the project.
- We value safety—it's safe to be yourself, let your voice be heard, ask questions, take risks, make mistakes and learn from them.

These beliefs and values are reflected in how teachers and students talk, how they treat each other, and how they work during a project. They use positive and empowering language. They seek to understand each other. They are not satisfied with first drafts; they refer to quality criteria and welcome feedback. They do not go with the easy answer or solution, but look for additional possibilities.

You can also find evidence of beliefs and values in what you see on the classroom walls. You might see artifacts such as a set of shared norms, a list of student-generated questions, samples of student work, rubrics, slogans on posters, and sentence stems for discussions.

Building Culture Through Norm-Setting

Norms, which some teachers prefer to call "community agreements," are another foundation of a PBL culture. They are a set of universally accepted and understood guidelines to follow when working together or sharing the same space.

Consider this way of thinking about norms and culture, from PBLWorks's Sarah Field:

"Every classroom has a culture and every classroom has norms regardless of whether they are intentional—and when they are not intentional they usually replicate the culture and norms and power dynamics of our larger society. So being purposeful and explicit and transparent about norms and culture with students is a way of making the implicit explicit and ensuring that the norms in your classroom really align to what you believe about learning."

Community agreements differ from traditional "classroom rules" set by a teacher, as you can tell from these four criteria for effective norms and their use:

1. **Co-created with students**

    Norms that govern a classroom environment should be the product of the inhabitants of the environment, not just one person. Co-creating these norms reinforces the expectation that everyone, teacher and students alike, share the responsibility for what goes on during the course of a project. (See the sample set of co-created norms on the next page.)

2. **Clearly understood**

    Effective norms are exactly what they sound like: a normal part of your class and used routinely during a project. Students shouldn't have to figure them out or uncover them as they go; they should be pre-arranged, and taught (through modeling, among other strategies) so that all students understand and can meet what is expected of them. School culture and norms may be different from those at students' homes—which is fine, as long as you are open with students about why and how they differ.

3. **The shared responsibility of students and the teacher**

   With practice and experience, students internalize norms and will remind each other about them. The role of the teacher is to facilitate their formation and provide reminders when appropriate. This may sound like just another form of teacher behavior policing, but these reminders can come in the form of team work agreements and visual references posted around the room. Norms can also be part of any direct instruction that takes place during a project or when students begin project work time. Norms and routines that are well-articulated and used regularly diminish the need for a teacher to act as a "class watchman."

4. **Revisited and revised**

   Norms may need to be revised periodically to make sure they stay relevant to the class and its changing dynamics. Your classroom during week two looks and acts very differently than your classroom in week 14. Revisiting and revising norms helps ensure these agreements speak to the culture in the room at that moment.

WE RESPECT EACH OTHER.

WE LISTEN TO EACH OTHER'S IDEAS AND SHARE OUR OWN.

WE SHOW UP ON TIME AND READY TO WORK.

WE ARE PROBLEM SOLVERS.

WE HAVE A GROWTH MINDSET.

Putting norms into action: 5 tools and strategies

Here are some examples of activities to help students generate norms and reflect on their use:

Classroom Constitution

At the beginning of the year, create a class-generated "constitution" with norms and guidelines for following them. This is a great way to formally establish norms and create a shared sense of ownership and responsibility for your learners. Display a piece of chart paper or a Google Doc and ask the class to describe an effective environment for learning and working together. As they give descriptors, follow up with, "And what can we all agree to do to make sure that happens?" By the end of the conversation, you'll have your starting norms.

Team/Class Agreements

If a whole-class discussion doesn't seem like the best approach, have students in their project teams do the above activity, focusing on creating a list that describes the team culture they would like to see. At the end of the small group discussions, have teams report out on the norms they generated, while you create a list. Every time a norm is repeated, add an extra checkmark, creating a "heat map" to show which norms are the biggest priorities for the class, then use them to form the class-wide list. This is a good activity to show students that while there are some norms that should be a part of every activity, there are others they may want to add just for their groups—which gives them the sense of agency that's so important in PBL.

Ideal Teammate

If you are interested in a longer, more introspective process, have each student do a quick-write to describe their ideal teammate. Ask them to talk about characteristics, dispositions, interests, or things they want people they work with to do. Post them for a gallery walk (or use an online discussion board like Padlet) and ask students to look for common descriptors. Use them for the creation of your norms list.

Checking Back In: Thumbs Up

Display a list of the agreed-upon norms by standing in front of the list and pointing to each norm one by one. Ask students to show thumbs up, down, or sideways indicating how they think the class is doing with this norm. Students can use this same process in their project teams.

Checking Back In: Exit Ticket Glows and Grows

Have students reflect on norms in an exit ticket, identifying their "glows and grows"—one norm they feel is going really well, and another they feel needs improvement. You can then use part of the next class to do an activity or team builder that helps them address the gaps they identified.

PBL PRO TIP

Not All Norms Fit Every Student

When setting norms for the whole class, or when teams add their own norms, be aware that agreements that work really well for most students may be very challenging for some. For example, "Speak up and share your ideas during discussions" might be hard for shy or socially challenged students, or those who need longer processing time. Accordingly, coach students to create norms that include respect for different learning/thinking/work preferences, and avoid a simple "majority rule" approach when reaching agreement on them.

Building Culture Through Protocols and Routines

Though every project is unique, a shared understanding among your students about "how we do things in this class" helps create a culture that will help them succeed in any project. Routines give students the predictability they need to navigate a multi-part project while staying focused on the learning goals. Protocols and routines also promote equitable participation and meaningful and efficient communication.

Routines will also make your project significantly easier to manage, which we'll say more about in the next chapter. When building routines into your class, prioritize those that can be used across multiple projects, such as feedback protocols, research methods, discussion protocols, and formative assessment practices.

Though it may seem counter-intuitive, the consistency and repeatability of routines enables flexibility for the teacher. For example, let's say you realize that there is an emerging misunderstanding or a common curiosity emerging among students. The ability to say to your students, "Hey, there seems to be a cool idea popping up in some teams, let's set up the room for a quick 10 minute two-to-one fishbowl and explore it" or "I'm seeing a common error emerging, let's do a quick gallery walk," and have students understand the expectations around setup and engagement enables the opportunity to take rich dives into necessary—or serendipitous—learning opportunities.

Using routines to reinforce norms

Routines and shared practices play a central role in the development and realization of classroom norms. A typical example is, "We treat one another with respect." This is a norm no one would argue with, but how does a norm like this become realized in a classroom? The answer is by having classroom routines and practices that breathe life into it.

For instance, sentence starters for how to respectfully disagree might be on the wall for students to refer to during discussions, such as "I see your point, but I wonder if…?" or "I have a different perspective…"

In addition, exit tickets or other periodic quick-writes might be centered around the idea of respecting one's peers, prompting students to reflect on a moment during class when they might have felt respected by a classmate, or a moment of outward respect that they witnessed. Creating routines and practices that support your norms, and then making that connection explicit to students, will help build a classroom environment that supports independent and accountable students.

Some routines that build culture are also used in more traditional classrooms, and are especially valuable for PBL classrooms, such as:

Thinking & discussion routines

Use routines that reinforce classroom values and norms when students read a text, think about and exchange ideas, or discuss something, such as "See, Think, Wonder" and "Think, Pair, Share." (For more, check out Harvard's Project Zero at visiblethinkingpz.org.).

Starters & closers

Begin class with routines that get students thinking about and sharing aloud what they're going to do today and how it connects to particular norms. End class by bringing everyone back together with a look back on how norms were used or reflected in what they did.

Celebrations

All throughout a project, look for things to celebrate, and ask students to do this too. It might be a norm having to do with "growth mindset"—have a shout-out when you or a student sees someone overcoming a challenge or learning something new. Or it might be a norm around "helping each other"—do a fist-bump to recognize it when it happens.

Some Final Thoughts

We'd like to leave this chapter by reiterating the importance of three keys to building the right culture for PBL. They run as a theme through much of the advice and ideas we've given. Always keep them in mind as you deepen your practice as a PBL teacher, and as you read the other chapters in this book:

❯ **Relationships:** How can you better know your students, and form closer ties with and among them?

❯ **Independence:** How can you encourage and support students in becoming self-directed learners?

❯ **Ownership:** How can you build a sense of agency in students, and get them to see a project as theirs, not yours?

CHAPTER 4

Managing Activities

WELL-MANAGED PBL CLASSROOMS, AS WE SAID in the last chapter, look and feel different from a classroom dominated by traditional instruction.

Instead of students sitting dutifully in their seats, listening to a lecture and taking notes or absorbing as much as they can through activities rooted in compliance, with PBL you would often see students working independently as the teacher circulates.

Students might be working in small teams, in pairs, or individually, utilizing resources as needed, checking in with peers or the teacher when the need arises. Or they could be engaging in more structured activities, but are not led every step of the way by the teacher.

The teacher, free from having to lead the learning every minute from the front of the room, can devote the majority of their time to monitoring and coaching student interactions, giving one-on-one help to individuals or teams, or providing differentiated support.

This kind of environment is not created magically, or overnight. It's the result of what we talked about in the last chapter: building the right classroom culture, and the careful use of management tools and strategies, which we'll discuss in this chapter.

"Manage Activities" in the Project Based Teaching Rubric:

- The classroom features an appropriate mixture of individual and team work time, whole group and small group instruction.
- Classroom routines and norms are consistently followed during project work time to maximize productivity.
- Project management tools (group calendar, contract, learning log, etc.) are used to support student self-management and independence.
- Realistic schedules, checkpoints, and deadlines are set but flexible; no bottlenecks impede workflow.
- Well-balanced teams are formed according to the nature of the project and student needs, with appropriate student voice and choice.

It's about structure

Sir Ken Robinson said, "Every farmer or gardener knows you cannot make a plant grow. The plant grows itself. What you do is provide the conditions for growth." This is a good way to think about managing a PBL unit. Just as a gardener doesn't just scatter seeds in the ground and hope for the best, a PBL teacher carefully sets up classroom structures and routines and monitors progress to help ensure students complete a project successfully.

Classroom structures include both the physical arrangement of the room (or online space) and the norms and routines that guide students' learning and smooth the process of doing work. Establishing effective structures that work across all of your projects helps keep them from becoming cumbersome and maintain focus on the learning goals.

Setting up your classroom space

In setting up your classroom space for PBL, first consider what resources students will need as the project progresses, then make those available in the classroom. These could range from text-based resources and technology to physical artifacts, laboratory equipment, or hand tools. Also plan for team work, by arranging tables or ways to put desks together.

In many PBL classrooms, you might find the current project's driving question prominently displayed, as well as students' need to know questions, rubrics, sample work or drafts, or other evidence of student inquiry. A project wall or a project corner might

PBL PRO TIP

Create a Project Website

Setting up a project website might seem intimidating, but there are many great resources for easily building and managing your own website. Additionally, you likely already have a student who knows how and is willing to teach you or set it up and manage it themselves—with you as their client. Also, a website requires very little upkeep, and can be reused or repurposed easily year to year (as opposed to physically setting up and replacing a physical project wall or corner).

have copies of all relevant documents such as rubrics, calendars, time sheets, task logs, group agreements, role descriptions, and resource lists (to name just a few). This project wall might also be a website, so students can have access to all of their documents as well as additional materials such as multimedia resources, and classroom photos. Designing your classroom space to maximize student independence not only helps students develop those skills, but it also simplifies your ability to manage day-to-day activities and focus on your students and their learning.

PBL PRO TIP

Handling the "What Did I Miss?" Question when Students Are Absent

Imagine a student approaches you asking: "I was absent yesterday. What did I miss?" How would you answer? Your answer to this question might say a lot about how your classroom is managed. Do you go to your laptop and gather materials they missed, then explain yesterday's agenda? Do you send them to another student or their team? What if instead they could simply go to a file box with a labeled folder for each class period containing an agenda, copy of notes, and any other materials from that day? The "file box" could also be an online repository— a class website or the school's Learning Management System.

Establishing Management Routines

Teacher and author Lucy Calkins, in describing the "writing workshop," makes a point that applies to managing a PBL classroom:

"It is significant to note that the most creative environments in our society are not ever-changing ones. The artist's studio, the researcher's laboratory, the scholar's library, is each deliberately kept simple so as to support the complexities of the work-in-progress. They are deliberately kept predictable so the unpredictable can happen."

Protocols and thinking routines provide structure for making student-student interactions more purposeful and efficient. Predictable routines help to streamline management processes in a PBL classroom. Routines also help make time in a project—which there often doesn't seem to be enough of—more effective, because they reduce the cognitive load for students in figuring out what is going on and what they are supposed to be doing.

Here are some examples of routines that help make common scenarios more efficient (and in turn, maximize learning time).

Common Scenario or Classroom Activity	Sample Routine
Beginning and ending class	"Check In, Check Out": Begin or end the class with a team check-in question. This might include revisiting the project's need to know questions, identifying or reflecting on learning and work goals for the day, or checking in on norms.
Transitioning between independent/small group/ large group configurations	Teach explicit cues for these transitions and practice the transitions with students. Use visible cues (e.g., a sign or dial at the front of the room) to indicate the type of interaction happening at a given time, and the expected behaviors for it.
Distributing and/or collecting project materials	Have one member of each team serve a particular organizational role, such as materials manager, for the duration of the project. Set aside a specific place in the room where all project materials are located so that students can find and return materials easily.
Seeking help when a group or individual is "stuck" during work time	Implement an "ask three before you ask me" policy. Set up a "help desk" or "office hours" queue/sign up sheet.
Pausing a work process to check in about working agreements or norms	Teach students to use (or have them create) a structured step-by-step process for calling a time-out, checking in regarding process, and returning to work. Be sure this process is visible in the classroom for quick reference.
Checking for consensus/ making decisions	Use a "fist to five" process to check in on agreements regarding a proposed idea. If student perspectives vary, have them share their ideas in structured rounds.

Managing Workflow with Checkpoints

As students progress through a project, it's inevitable that they will proceed at different paces. This can be an unsettling prospect for both teachers and students who are accustomed to environments where everyone is moving through the learning at the same time. However, embedding structured checkpoints throughout your project can go a long way toward easing that concern and provide clarity with the project's workflow.

You'll find that project checkpoints are mutually beneficial to both you and your students:

For teachers, checkpoints:	For students, checkpoints:
Guide planning	Support growth toward independence with self-management skills
Provide multiple opportunities to formatively assess and provide feedback	Maintain engagement and momentum by breaking the project down into smaller achievable steps
Allow for quick and visible tracking of student progress	Promote high-quality work and achievement of learning outcomes

Project checkpoints can range in formality and take many forms, including:

- Quick check-ins
- Teacher conferences
- Peer feedback sessions
- Student discussion protocols

- Self-assessments
- Goal-setting and action steps
- Interviews
- Polls and quizzes

As you explore your options, consider how checkpoints will ensure students have opportunities to show their learning, both in terms of academic content and success skills, as well as show their progress on completing project tasks.

As you develop and use checkpoints with your students, consider these questions:

- At what moments in your project will it be most important to include checkpoints to assess progress?
- How might you involve students in the development of checkpoints?
- How will you make the checkpoints visible and clear for all students?
- How might you deal with students who are not meeting checkpoints on time?

Using project management tools

PBL teachers and students use a variety of project management tools to scaffold independence, ensure quality work, and provide workflow efficiency. It's also a great way to introduce students to project management tools that professionals use in the world outside of school.

Some quick internet research will uncover a few tools you might try, including:

- Kanban Boards
- Scrum boards
- Burndown Charts

PBL PRO TIP

Checkpoints as "Rites of Passage"

Social studies teacher Eric White was frustrated by the "race to the finish line" approach that he allowed in projects. This usually resulted in careless work that made presentation days underwhelming. In an effort to more accurately track student progress and better provide quality control, Eric started using "Rites of Passage" with his students.

"Rites of Passage represented the transition students would take from one phase of a project to the next. In order to move forward the next phase of a project, students had to prove they were ready. This proof usually involved a draft of work and a teacher conference," the veteran PBL teacher explains.

On the next page is a PBL Rites of Passage handout Eric created for his "Historical Music Video Project," which challenged students to create an original music video for a song that reflected and affected American society at the time it was written. Students also wrote an essay on the historical context and significance of the song as an accompaniment to the video. With multiple products involved in the project, it was important for students to know exactly where they were and where they were going.

Eric further explained how the Rites of Passage approach promoted revision and a growth mindset with students. "If students were not approved to move forward on their first try, it did not mean they failed or lost points. It simply meant they were not ready yet. 'Yet' was critical to maintaining motivation with the Rites of Passage. 'Yet' meant an opportunity for students to revise and improve without fear of having their grade suffer. 'Yet' also meant that I needed to scaffold, differentiate, and personalize my support to meet students where they were."

PBL Rites of Passage Sheet
The Historical Music Video Project

Course: United States History

NAME: _____

CLASS PERIOD: _____

Rite of Passage	Feedback/Revisions /Celebrations	Approval Signature
1. Song Defense		
2. Essay Outline		
3. Rough Draft		
4. Final Draft		
5. Music Video Pitch		
6. Storyboard		
7. Video Rough Draft		
8. Video Final Draft		

Forming and Managing Student Teams

For students, one of the most challenging aspects of PBL can be working in teams; for teachers, it's managing the work of teams. As even adults know, working collaboratively is not something you "master"—there's always more to learn and ways to grow, and issues can arise even in experienced groups. That said, "collaboration" is an important success skill, and students can develop it through PBL much more effectively than they can with typical traditional instructional methods, so let's look at how to make it work as well as possible during a project.

What Collaboration Is NOT

"Students gain collaborative skills by contributing to the learning and work of others and building upon each other's ideas to *co-create...* not by just dividing and conquering tasks to complete the final product." That's how teacher Aaron Eisberg put it in his blog post *Why Collaboration Is More Than "Group Work"* at pblworks.org. Many students, and sometimes teachers, view collaboration as simply divvying up the pieces of a project to do individually, then putting it all together at the end. Instead, Eisberg recommends managing student teams to help them be "interactive, innovative, and interdependent"—that's true collaboration.

First ask: when should students work in teams?

Not all tasks are equal in terms of potential for collaboration. While having students review for a quiz in a small group may be useful, it's not necessarily the kind of task that leads to deep learning through peer interaction. According to Elizabeth Cohen and Rachel Lotan (2014), tasks that are appropriate for group work should be:

- Not easily answered; multi-dimensional
- Interesting and relevant to students
- Require multiple modalities such as reading, writing, sight, sound, or multimedia
- Challenging and rewarding for students

Sounds a lot like PBL, doesn't it?

Keep these criteria in mind as you think about forming and managing teams. The project as a whole, if it includes the Essential Elements of Gold Standard PBL, meets the criteria—but not all activities need to be done in teams. Many PBL teachers, when they first start doing projects, assume students should be working in project teams from the get-go. It's a common conception, but a more advanced practice is to consider what kinds of teams are necessary, and when.

For example, you may have students work in a "core" project team to develop their final answers to a driving question and major products, but not form this team right away or do all activities within it. It depends on the project's length and complexity, too. For shorter and simpler projects, having students work in one project team might be just fine.

It can be helpful to form short-term groupings—either random groups, interest-based groups, or groups focused on learning a targeted skill—for particular learning activities within the project, such as:

- Reteaching complex concepts
- Pre-teaching technical vocabulary
- Mini-workshop sessions
- Challenging/extending understanding for those who already know the core content
- Role-alike groups to "compare notes" or troubleshoot during a project
- Self-selected/opt-in workshops on various topics/skills
- Expert teams to learn something and bring it back to their team, aka "jigsawing"
- Workshops designed to address targeted skills that were identified needs for some students based on teacher or self-assessment
- Feedback protocols

Forming teams

Like many things in PBL, there is no hard and fast rule for forming student teams. It depends on you, your students, and the project. Here are some considerations:

1. **How big will your teams be?**

   For most projects, a team size of three to four students allows for a fair distribution of work and supports the development of interpersonal skills without being logistically overwhelming. A pair is not quite a team; there's some collaboration, certainly, but not as many perspectives and ideas, or opportunities to practice real-world project management skills. And for most "main course" projects, there is simply too much for two people to do. You might consider teams of five or more students for projects with highly complex products that require more work and expertise, although large teams can make things like communication, division of tasks, and interpersonal dynamics more challenging.

2. **How much choice will students have in selecting teammates?**

   How you approach this may depend on the age and experience level of your students. Will you decide on teams for students? Will you make this decision with input from students? Or will you support students in a process of selecting their own teams? Greater student input may increase buy-in, but be sure students make wise choices. For example, working with their best friend may not be a good idea, and students may not recognize or see the value of what some of their peers might bring to a project. Experienced PBL students may be able to form their own effective teams, but even then some students may feel left out or gaps in strengths might arise, so coach them in this process.

3. **What aspects of the project design might inform teaming?**
   Take into account the particular skills, experiences, or perspectives that are relevant to the project. For example, if the project involves video game design, you'll want to ensure that each team includes students with a lot of video game experience.

4. **What do you know about the strengths, interests, and needs of your students?**
   There are many ways to learn about your students, and your knowledge of students (along with their self-knowledge) should help to inform the creation of diverse and well-balanced teams. As you form teams, consider how you can give students opportunities to leverage their known strengths while also inviting them to develop and demonstrate new knowledge and skills.

Tips for Forming Teams

- Have students form interest-based teams focused on the project content. For example, in a project focused on addressing problems in the community, students might choose their teams based on their interest in focusing on transportation, housing, health, etc.

- Have each student complete an index card listing the names of up to four students with whom they can be productive, and one person with whom they cannot be productive (this could be a best friend, a student with whom they have a personal conflict, etc.). Team each student with at least one "productive" partner, and avoid teaming students who self-identify as less-productive pairs.

- Identify the characteristics you want balanced across each team (e.g., big picture thinkers and detail-oriented thinkers, introverts and extroverts). Have students self-identify according to these characteristics, then self-select or teacher-assign teams that include a balance of characteristics.

- As you plan projects across a semester or school year, vary the teams across projects so students have an opportunity to work with different people.

Assigning roles

Having clear team roles is a familiar project management strategy in adult workplaces. Intentional design and assignment of roles enhances collaboration for students by increasing authenticity, engagement, and accountability, and builds leadership skills.

Students could have a hand in choosing their roles, especially if they're experienced with PBL, but there are advantages—with equity implications—to assigning roles as their teacher. Assigning roles allows the teacher to distribute opportunities across the classroom and avoid reinforcing students' existing perceptions of who is a leader, or the academic expert, or "the artistic one." Also keep in mind that skills and characteristics that teachers might typically rely on while grouping students such as public speaking and leadership are not innate; they are developed in places like school. Accordingly, our grouping strategies ought to give every student the same opportunity to practice their leadership or public communication skills.

PBL PRO TIP

Use a Learner Profile to Form Teams

The SING Learner Profile below (adapted from the Denver Public Schools) can be used to solicit information from students that you can use to form teams and roles:

Strengths: What do you know you are great at?

Interests: What lights your fire?

Needs: What structures and supports do you need in order to work effectively?

Goals: In what areas of work and learning do you want to grow?

After you've collected this information, ask: How do students' SING profile results mesh with the roles you've created for the project? How do the assignments help students demonstrate and share their known strengths?

Equity Issues in Team Work

Decades of work from researchers Elizabeth Cohen and Rachel Lotan (Cohen and Lotan, 2014) have illustrated the ways in which group work can create a more equitable classroom, as well as how group work can create unequal learning opportunities that mirror and reinforce existing social inequalities.

The problem, as the authors describe it, is that hierarchies emerge in groups and the status ordering of these small groups tends to align with local status characteristics such as academic ability (real or perceived) and peer status, as well as social characteristics such as gender, race, class, and nationality. As the hierarchies emerge in small groups, students' status "out there" tends to become a self-fulfilling prophecy within the group as lower-status students' participation and learning potential are impacted. In other words, failing to address status and inequity in our classroom grouping strategies makes it more likely that our classroom culture reflects and perpetuates wider social inequalities.

Given this, teachers have an obligation to design for, monitor, and intervene around issues of status during group work. Cohen and Lotan lay out how to solve these problems along three dimensions: the design of the task, teacher moves during the task, and the classroom norms that support and structure.

Teacher Moves to Promote Equity in Team Work

Before beginning or planning team work, one of the first things any teacher should consider is what existing feelings and prejudices they have toward students. Teachers might consider particular students as "helpful" or "disruptive" or might make overly limited assumptions about students' motivation levels, or their academic and leadership abilities. We know that students believe, internalize, and often realize teachers' and their peers' expectations of them. It is imperative that teachers challenge their preconceptions of students as well as students' preconceptions of each other, so as not to create self-fulfilling prophecies for students.

During team work time in a project, teachers should monitor groups for verbal and visual signs of unequal participation and intervene using a practice Cohen refers to as *assigning competence*. Here's a summary of the practice, which is part of the "Complex Instruction" (CI) model Cohen, Lotan, and their colleagues at Stanford University developed as a way to address the learning needs of heterogeneous groups of learners:

> "CI invites more equitable student participation by assigning competence to students that helps to equalize status issues. In assigning competence, teachers pay attention to the things that low status students do well that move the group forward in the task. He or she then tells the students what they did well and the ways in which their contribution was important to their group. This serves the purpose of elevating students' status in their groups. When students are on a more equal footing in terms of how they are perceived by the group, they are more likely to participate." (Cheyne, 2014)

Your goal should be to form effective teams by creating and assigning roles based on delegation and task oversight rather than roles that require a single person to take on all of the work for a particular product. For example, you may have heard of commonly used roles like "materials manager" or "team leader." As you design roles ask yourself the following questions: Are the responsibilities of each role equal? Do the roles you create ask students to help each other with product creation? Do the team roles enhance project work? Do these roles reflect real world work? Consider shifting roles from "doer" roles (e.g., team leader, artist) to "delegator" roles (e.g., project manager, creative director).

Fostering a culture of collaboration

We discuss the topic of building the right culture for PBL in Chapter 3, but let's look specifically at managing student teams within that culture.

Here are some activities to help create a "culture of collaboration" in your classroom:

- With students, identify a behavior or behaviors that might improve team work—for example, "disagree respectfully" or "build on each other's ideas." Co-create a definition with students and post it in the classroom.
- Give students the opportunity to critically observe, label, and discuss the new behaviors in an objective and academic way.
- Ask students to reflect on their own development and growth regarding the new behaviors.
- Discuss or co-create a collaboration rubric (find an example at pblworks.org) so students understand what good and not-so-good teamwork looks like, and ask students to use the rubric at check-ins to reflect on how they're doing.
- Have students create and sign a "team contract" that spells out how they agree to act, how they will handle problems that arise, how they will work together, and so on. You could provide a template or they could create one from scratch (find examples at pblworks.org).
- Use formal discussion protocols such as Socratic seminars and their debriefs as a tool for working on behaviors such as connecting to another person's comments or understanding before disagreeing.

- Do team-building activities such as design or construction challenges, being sure to incorporate and develop specific behaviors such as inviting new ideas from teammates or building on another person's ideas. Include targeted reflection or other post-activity discussion to reflect on such questions as:
  - What did your team accomplish?
  - Did everyone participate? Would everyone in your group agree?
  - Did everyone in the group have a chance to speak and be heard?
  - Did you ask questions of your group members?
  - Can you describe how your group members were thinking about (the task/content)?
  - What did we do that other teams could learn from?
  - What team actions could we improve upon?

Managing Time

There seems to never be enough time, and we can't magically create more. However, with a few important shifts in our practice, we can make the time we invest in PBL both impactful and efficient.

Let's review some strategies and structures that will produce a return on the investment of time in PBL. We'll start with three pieces of advice:

1. **Don't make PBL mainly an at-home experience.**

    When the tyranny of the urgent sets in, this can be a very tempting option. However, PBL simply cannot be done well if most project work is done outside of class. Both the learning process and product development should happen during class time, and as the teacher you need to play an active role in it. In-class activities include (but aren't limited to):

    - Asking questions and identifying resources to answer questions
    - Brainstorming ideas
    - Collaboration with other students and stakeholders
    - Lessons and scaffolds to acquire key content and skills
    - Creation of products
    - Critique and revision of products
    - Formative and summative assessments
    - Moments of reflection to capture learning

    The list could go on. The takeaway is that PBL is much too comprehensive and meaningful to simply send home and forget. Sure, some small slices of project work could happen away from class, but making time for PBL is important. We must resist the shortcuts that don't pay off.

2. **No ambiguous project work time.**

    Instead of sending students directly into work time with their teams, provide opportunities for students to be able to productively self-manage that time. Ask them to plan their use of time by giving them prompts to discuss before officially entering into project work time, such as:

    - What are our team goals for work time today?
    - How will I individually contribute toward our team goals?
    - How will we know when we've achieved our team and individual goals?
    - What evidence will we be able to show for the time we've spent today?
    - If our progress stalls, what strategies will we use to get back on track?

Remember to provide time for students to debrief at the end of their work time as well, with prompts such as:

- In what ways did our team reach or fall short of our goals for work time?
- How did I individually contribute/not contribute to our team goals?
- What evidence have we produced that accurately shows what we achieved during work time?
- Based on our progress, what are our new goals?
- What are our most important next steps moving forward?

3. **Stay structured and student-centered by giving regular lessons.**

   Yes, we still can have structured daily, or almost daily, lessons in PBL that address key learning targets in your curriculum. This is great news for those who are wondering about the messiness of PBL and how it may impact time management. Below are two suggestions to keep your daily lessons focused and student-centered while allowing you to maximize your time.

The workshop model

The Workshop Model (first designed by Lucy Calkins and further developed by Samantha Bennett) provides a simple and proven structure that maximizes student work time, practice, and reflection. It also allows the teacher time to provide mini-lessons, clarify misconceptions, and scaffold as needed. The time a workshop takes can vary, from around 30 minutes to 1–2 hours, but it has three basic parts:

- *Mini-Lesson:* The teacher provides some direct instruction with the entire class. You could review previous learning, share and unpack learning targets, introduce a new concept or skill, or check in with the project's driving question and need to know list of questions. Generally, the mini-lesson represents 20–25% of the overall time.
- *Work Time:* Students could engage in a variety of activities, such as individual and team practice, reading, research, peer feedback, and development of work drafts. The teacher is able to maximize time and impact through strategic listening, conferring with individuals or small groups, differentiating instruction, and providing feedback. Misconceptions can be clarified and other feedback can be provided through short "catch and release" moments with the whole group. The teacher may pause work time briefly to redirect or provide new information. Generally, work time represents 50–60% of the overall time.

- *Debrief:* The debrief includes time to come back as a whole group to revisit the driving question, need to know list, and learning targets. Students have opportunities to reflect and teachers may conduct formative assessment. Generally, the debrief represents 15–20% of the overall time.

The Workshop Structure

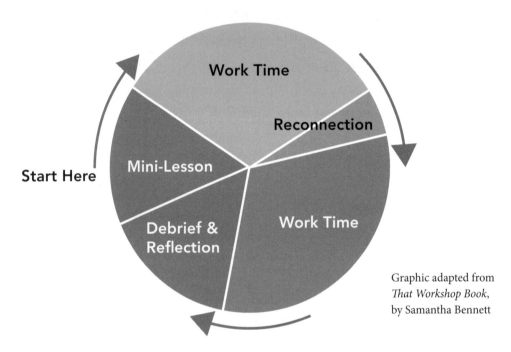

Graphic adapted from *That Workshop Book,* by Samantha Bennett

Learning stations

Time-strapped teachers will find plenty of opportunities to personalize their support of students through learning stations, which include various tasks and activities that small groups of students rotate through. Some of the tasks are completed in small teams or individually, and the work is designed to support student learning in the project. Stations are intended to be self-managed by students, although there could be a station led by the teacher as well. Learning station work might include online and offline activities, such as:

- Reading
- Discussion
- Observation
- Practicing a skill
- Research
- Games

- Physical Movement
- Listening
- Simulations
- Lab Work
- Extension or Remediation

PBL PRO TIP

Share Information with Teams Without Pausing Work Time

If students have roles in their teams, you can use them to share up-to-date information with teams without stopping all the work in the room. For example, if there is a change in the requirements for a model or design, ask for a quick meeting with the "product engineers." Has the due date for a deliverable changed? Ask to see the "project managers." This way you can deliver the information you need to the people who need it, and other team members can continue their work.

Keeping the Pace with PBL

One of the biggest challenges PBL teachers face is staying on track with time and setting realistic but flexible schedules, checkpoints, and deadlines. Lots of things can quickly turn your project plan into a traffic jam, from unforeseen interruptions to tech problems to snow days to pep rallies. Or you might find you need to reteach a concept, rethink a project's major product, or simplify or shorten certain aspects of the project. Below are a few tips from teachers who are conquering their project calendars.

1. **Set a Deadline You Can't (or Won't) Extend**

   While you might have flexibility with some deadlines, set a final presentation day that is firm. One surefire way to guarantee the finish line of your project isn't constantly extended is to send a "Save the Date" invite to your public audience ahead of time. This might feel intimidating, but it will help you prioritize what matters most and maintain a healthy amount of productive tension. The bottom line is that a project will take as long as you say it takes, so go ahead and set that date!

2. **Kill Your Darlings**

   This is age-old advice for writers. To preserve integrity and move the story forward, an author must sometimes cut their most prized passages. Just like writers, we can sometimes grow overly attached to our activities and lessons. They may be interesting and even fun for students, but could stray from the main focus of the project. To stay on track, these "darlings" must be cut. Remember, every movie has deleted scenes to keep it coherent or compact; your project may need the same.

3. Flip Your Classroom

Lectures can consume a large amount of class time, so consider using a flipped approach. Lectures can be recorded (or found online, done by others) and assigned as homework, which can free up class time for personalized support, deeper discussions, and application of the concepts discussed in the videos.

Managing Presentations

We discussed some aspects of the public product on pages 53-54, such as who students will share their work with and in what format. We noted that not all projects need to end with a formal presentation to an audience, but if you are having such an event, here are some tips for managing it:

- Consider involving students in planning and running the event.
- Set a date and invite audiences well in advance. If families are going to attend, hold events during a time when most are able to—perhaps holding one during daytime hours and another in the evening.
- If you plan on having audience members question students, or assess them and provide feedback, provide a project overview, a checklist or simple rubric, and sample questions to ask students. Make sure to include some "deep" questions about, say, the driving question and how their thinking evolved, or how they used success skills during the project. (See an example of a "Project Presentation Audience Feedback Form" at my.pblworks.org/resources.)
- If students are observing each other's presentations, remind them how to be a good audience and consider giving them a task, such as taking notes on key points and questions, assessing or giving feedback.
- At science fair or museum exhibit types of events, consider having some student teams make a presentation to the whole group at the beginning, to set the stage for the event and share project details. Then audience members can roam around the room, discussing projects with students.
- Download the "Presentation Day Checklist" at my.pblworks.org/resources to help you organize what you will need to have ready before the big day.

If you're not having a formal presentation—for example, if students create a website or publish a book online—be sure to provide ways for the public/readers/end-users to ask questions, engage with students, or at least give feedback. Include a place where students explain the process they used to do the project, and their reflections on it.

Finally, don't neglect the need to have a celebration at the end of a project—see more on that in Chapter 7, "Engaging and Coaching Students."

FOR REMOTE LEARNING **Tech Tools for Managing Activities**

These are some that are currently available, although more are always being created.

Screencastify, Edpuzzle: For a "flipped classroom" approach, teachers can record lectures and have students watch them prior to arriving at class, ensuring that class time is spent more effectively. Edpuzzle also allows formative checks to be inserted into videos, providing data for teachers on the effectiveness of the learning resources they are selecting.

Flipgrid: To help manage online discussions, students can create and share short videos.

Google Keep, Kanbanchi, Trello: Google Keep allows teachers or students to share task lists that can be edited in real time, allowing teams to stay connected to what is being done and what needs to be accomplished. Kanbanchi and Trello are virtual scrum boards where students can track their progress and teachers can designate milestones and time frames.

Jamboard, Padlet: To help with organizing work time, use these two "bulletin board" apps to allow students to self-select a goal or focus for their work time by posting their name and current task. Also a good way to have students visually request help.

Some Final Thoughts

❯ Managing time in a project can be a constant challenge, so don't get down on yourself if you go a bit long with your first few attempts. Being a great PBL teacher doesn't take perfection; it takes reflection. You'll get more efficient as you progress with the practice, so continue to iterate and learn.

❯ The time used in a project should emphasize *learning* and *process* over product. As Ron Ritchart noted in his book *Creating Cultures of Thinking,* avoid the trap of falling into a work-oriented vs. a learning-oriented culture. Instead of focusing mainly on task completion, focus on thinking and deep understanding.

CHAPTER 5

Assessing Student Learning

ASSESSMENT IN PROJECT BASED LEARNING IS A topic that often brings up a lot of questions.

Students may ask, how will I know how well I'm doing in a class if we're doing projects instead of the usual quizzes, tests, and homework assignments for points? What if I'm on a team and have to do more than my share of the work? (Or, others may wonder if they can get on a team with someone who will help them all earn a high grade.)

Teachers may ask similar questions, from their own perspective, and more: How can I assess individual learning when students are working as a team in a project? How do I assess content knowledge as well as success skills? Am I the only one doing the assessing? And what about grading? Is assessment so different in PBL that I have to reinvent my whole approach?

School leaders may ask additional questions, such as: To what extent, and how can we, share practices for assessment in PBL across teachers and departments? How does PBL fit within our school/district's assessment system? How can using PBL help us assess whether our students are ready to graduate?

"Assess Student Learning" in the Project Based Teaching Rubric:

> Project products and other sources of evidence are used to thoroughly assess subject-area standards as well as success skills.

> Individual student learning is adequately assessed, not just team-created products.

> Formative assessment is used regularly and frequently, with a variety of tools and processes.

> Structured protocols for critique and revision are used regularly at checkpoints; students give and receive effective feedback to inform instructional decisions and students' actions.

> Regular, structured opportunities are provided for students to self-assess their progress and, when appropriate, assess peers on their performance.

> Standards-aligned rubrics are used by students and the teacher throughout the project to guide both formative and summative assessment.

Parents may ask the same questions as students do, from their perspective: How will I know if my child is doing well in a lengthy project? What if my kid does most of the work on a team? What if my kid's grade suffers because of what their team did in a project?

This chapter will help answer these questions.

Assessment in a PBL Context

Before we dig into what assessment is like in PBL, let's review some basics of assessment generally.

Many educators hear the word "assessment" and think of tests. In recent years, since the No Child Left Behind (NCLB) era began and test-based accountability systems became the norm for many teachers, assessment might have a negative connotation. Teachers have had to prepare students for "benchmark assessments" at regular intervals during the school year, leading up to the high-stakes state tests each spring.

While testing has its place in measuring certain types of educational outcomes—and it can reveal inequities between subgroups of students and "raise the floor" for teaching practice—it has taken attention away from what assessment really is. It's about more than just measuring what students have learned; it's about improving their work in progress. This is the difference between summative assessment and formative assessment, which we explain more below in the context of PBL.

The concept of "balanced" assessment is good to keep in mind as you plan and implement projects. In addition to formative and summative assessment, you'll need to balance assessment of individual learning with work done in teams, and content knowledge and discipline-specific skills with the assessment of 21st century success skills. Assessment is done not only by the teacher, but also by students through self- and peer-assessment—and perhaps by outside experts or presentation audience members too.

Also think of balancing traditional forms of assessment (tests, quizzes, writing, assignments for points, etc.) with performance-based and other non-traditional kinds of assessment. There's a place for both in PBL; as is the case for scaffolding learning and managing the classroom, you don't need to throw away everything you already have in your teaching toolkit.

PBL PRO TIP

10 Best Practices in PBL Assessment

We gathered the following overall advice on assessment from PBLWorks National Faculty members. You'll see guidance on all of this and more in this chapter:

❯ Assess more, grade less.

❯ Informal assessment is important too; ask students to explain and reflect on what they're learning.

❯ Be transparent with students about assessment criteria and the process, and bring them into it.

❯ Allow student voice and choice in assessment, including differentiation of strategies.

❯ Make sure students understand, can use, and "own" the tools of assessment, such as rubrics.

❯ Assess success skills such as critical thinking, problem-solving, and collaboration, in addition to content knowledge.

❯ Be sure to assess individual learning and work, not just team-created products.

❯ Focus on feedback and formative assessment, and give students the opportunity to improve their work.

❯ Help parents and caregivers make a shift in their expectations for what assessment information is shared with them, beyond traditional grades.

❯ Broaden your thinking about who assesses; it's more powerful for students to hear a range of assessment voices, not only from the teacher but also peers, outside experts, and community members.

The Importance and Use of Formative Assessment

Formative assessment is especially important in PBL. Formative assessment *for* learning contrasts with summative assessment *of* learning, in the words of assessment expert Rick Stiggins. Here's a good way to understand the difference, with an analogy credited to Robert Stake at the University of Illinois: "When the cook tastes the soup, that's formative; when the guests taste the soup, that's summative." In PBL, with its emphasis on the process of learning and on creating high-quality public products, formative assessment plays a bigger role in your assessment plan than it typically does in traditional practice.

Our biggest message about formative assessment is this: use it to plan your teaching moves, with a focus on student growth. When you gather evidence from formative assessment, decide your next steps for providing instruction, resources, individual or small-group coaching, and other support. And involve students in the process, to build a student-centered culture and help them "own" their learning. Formative assessment also reinforces a growth mindset in students, helping them determine where they are and where they are going in the learning process.

Using Tech Tools for Formative Assessment

These tools work well for online or blended learning environments:

Google Classroom: This LMS allows teachers to easily create and differentiate formative checks, with a tool for giving private feedback to students.

Padlet/Jamboard: Students can post questions or comments about articles or lessons.

Flipgrid: Have students verbally check in on their learning or respond to a question of the day with an exit ticket. Teachers can respond to provide support.

Google Forms: Create short formative quizzes with this simple-to-use tool.

Edpuzzle: Take any video from YouTube or upload your own and insert formative checks throughout, which students must answer to progress through it.

Nearpod: Slide sharing capability with multiple formative tools included. Share short quizzes, open-ended reflections, and annotation tools with students.

In a typical heterogeneous classroom, the instruction following formative assessment may not be the same for all students. It's differentiated by need, and requires you to be flexible. You may decide to pull aside a small group to reteach a concept or skill, sit with one project team to help them overcome a collaboration challenge, or teach a previously taught concept to the entire class, but with a different approach. We'll say more about this in the next chapter, "Scaffolding Student Learning."

Use formative assessment frequently in a project. As we discussed in Chapter 1, "Designing and Planning a Project," your project calendar should have milestones on it—checkpoints where work-in-progress is assessed—but formative assessment should occur even more often. It doesn't always need to be an event or other formal process; simply walking around the room observing, or having a discussion with students, can be an opportunity for formative assessment. See the table below.

Informal Formative Assessment:	Formal Formative Assessment:
• exit tickets	• quizzes
• written reflections	• rough drafts
• observation	• short assignments
• thumbs up/down	• district benchmark assessments
• fist to five	• performance tasks
• online polls	• product checkpoints
• student check-ins	• student conferences
• analogy prompts	• critique protocols
• four corners	
• chalk talks	

(Note: Some of the above are explained in Chapter 4, "Managing Activities," or you can find them online.)

To plan what formative assessments you'll need, think about what information you want to get from them. Do you want to find out if students know some basic content or have some fundamental skills needed for the project? Then a quiz or short assignment might be sufficient. Do you need to see if they understand a concept? Ask them to explain it. To check if they've gained a critical thinking skill? Have them do a performance task, such as a reading/writing or problem-solving exercise where students can demonstrate the skill.

Feedback protocols

To promote student agency and ownership of assessment, teach them how to self-assess and do peer-assessment. Critique protocols are helpful tools for this—structured opportunities to give, receive, and apply peer feedback on their work in progress. Some protocols may also include feedback from experts, end-users of a product or service, students or adults beyond the classroom, or community members.

The protocol you choose depends on what kind of feedback students need at various stages of a project. How many you use, and how often, depends on the project—but generally it's a good idea to have students learn and regularly use two or three different protocols. There are many types of feedback protocols, which you can find online for implementation details, such as:

- Charrette
- Feedback Carousel
- Gallery Walk

- Praise, Question, Suggestion
- Tuning Protocol

FOR REMOTE LEARNING   **Doing Critique Protocols Online**

The feedback protocols above can work for remote learning and help ensure both active engagement and equity of voice.

Here are some tips and guidance:

> Make a timer visible to students, which helps them regulate the depth and speed at which they share ideas.

> Provide a graphic organizer for analyzing work, gathering thoughts, and giving and recording feedback.

> Structure the process to ensure that every student's/team's work is shared and receives feedback. You might create a Hyperdoc with links to each team's project, assign each student/team a specific slide in a shared deck like Google Slides, or have each student/team post their work to a designated Flipgrid or Padlet wall.

> Students can provide peer feedback to shared work by adding typed/ audio comments in SeeSaw; using Kaizena on Google Docs and Slides; by recording video comments in Canvas or Schoology; or using Flipgrid.

6 Tips for feedback protocols:

1. Refer to class norms or create a separate subset of norms for feedback protocols (e.g., Ron Berger's "be kind, specific, and helpful" guideline).
2. Teach students how to give effective feedback by modeling, providing sentence stems, practicing the process, etc.
3. Facilitate the project yourself, unless you have a deeply ingrained culture of critique and highly independent students who can introduce each step, provide prompts, and keep time.
4. Teach students how to think about and use feedback they receive. Let them know they don't need to respond or act upon every piece of feedback they got, just consider what was helpful.

Using Evidence from Projects to Assess "Graduate Profiles"

Many schools and districts have recently created a "graduate profile" that describes the skills and characteristics a student should have developed by 12th grade. These lists of desired learning outcomes typically include things like inquiry, citizenship, creativity, persistence, problem-solving, cultural competence, collaboration, communication, and more.

What's missing, according to Justin Wells of Envision Learning Partners, is how they are going to get there. He says,

> "Resist the impulse to start with the assessment question: How will we measure these skills? Instead, focus energy on what I call the practice question: How will our students practice these skills? (Wells, 2020)

We think one of the best ways to practice these skills is by regularly experiencing Project Based Learning. Then, if students collect evidence from projects over time in a "graduation portfolio," students and schools will have plenty to refer to when assessing whether they meet a graduate profile.

5. After a protocol, ask students to debrief the process. Discuss what went well, what could be improved, how well norms were followed, etc.

6. Allow time immediately after a feedback protocol for students to make plans for next steps.

Assessing Content Knowledge and Success Skills

Teachers know how to assess content knowledge and disciplinary skills, such as how to factor, write a persuasive essay, or design an experiment. You can still use many traditional assessment strategies for this purpose in PBL, as we said earlier.

In addition to using traditional tools to assess content knowledge in a project, you can assess it in the final product and supplemental material students complete. For example, you could add a row to a rubric for a project's major product, with indicators of evidence for content knowledge and the use of disciplinary skills. You could also assess understanding of key concepts by asking students to submit a written explanation of how they are demonstrated in the final product. For example, if a final product is a design for a building, students could annotate it to indicate how it shows evidence of achievement of learning targets.

Assessing success skills such as critical thinking, problem-solving, collaboration, communication, creativity, and project management might be new territory for teachers, however. They're seen as harder to measure in a "concrete" way and more subjective. Here again, think of assessment as part of a process for promoting student growth, not simply a means to determine a score or grade. Through assessment, you can encourage self-reflection and give students feedback on their use of success skills.

Here are some ideas to consider for assessing success skills in PBL:

- Use rubrics (such as those found at PBLWorks.org) or a set of criteria to capture specifically what it means to demonstrate the skill at various performance levels.

- Do not try to explicitly teach and assess too many success skills in one project. Focus on one or two, or even a part of one (e.g., one or two rows of a rubric) that align best with the particular project.

- Informally assess students when they use success skills through observation and discussion. Consider creating an "observation checklist" of particular success skills that you can use when observing teams.

- Ask questions during presentations to uncover students' use of success skills. For example, ask them to comment on how they solved problems or followed steps in project management.
- Provide regular opportunities for students to self-assess or peer-assess the use of success skills, referring to the rubric. Have them discuss their use of the skills in team debriefs. Consider having students collect and reflect on evidence using a journal or other documentation tool—or to avoid "journaling burnout" add these strategies to the mix:
  - Use technology tools such as a voice recorder or blog so students can record reflections and goals, and build on them throughout one or more projects.
  - Use cooperative reflection activities such as "Think, Pair, Share" or "Four Corners" as opportunities to think out loud and listen and learn from peers.
  - Have one group of students, perhaps representing various teams, engage in a "fishbowl" discussion while others observe and listen. Allow other students to move into and out of the discussion if they want to share their thinking.
  - Facilitate a whole-class Socratic seminar or Harkness discussion to share with and learn from one another.

Individual vs. Team Assessment

We've discussed the importance of learning how to work in teams as an important skill in the modern world. However, it raises questions for many newcomers to PBL with legitimate concerns about fairness when it comes to assessment. Students and parents often raise these concerns too, and school grading policies can also create challenges for assessing team-created work vs. individual work.

Here's our best advice for handling the issue, gleaned from the experience of veteran PBL teachers:

- When planning a project, include more individually done assignments and assessments than team-created work.
- In addition to a team-created product, have students write individual reports or other documentation to explain it in terms of the content and skills they learned.

- Ask students to regularly reflect on what they are learning and how they contributed to a team-created product, with evidence and/or a written explanation.
- If possible, require students to individually complete certain pieces of a team product (with input and feedback from teammates).

PBL PRO TIP

Grading in PBL

Grading varies a great deal from teacher to teacher, and you may have concerns about how it works in a project. If your school or district has a formal, required structure for grading, it may need to adapt to accommodate PBL. Here are some ideas to consider:

> Do not give one grade or a huge amount of points for the entire project; grade smaller assignments, quizzes and other assessments, and deliverables at checkpoints within the project.

> Base grades mostly on individual performance, not team-created work.

> Consider not grading team-created products at all, since students should still be motivated to do high-quality work by an engaging project and by sharing their work in public.

> Separate grades based on acquisition of content knowledge and skills from the assessment (and possibly grading) of success skills.

> Do not assign grades or points for the quality of work-in-progress or drafts; assign points for completion of project deliverables if you wish.

> Consider involving students in the process of determining fair grading practices. (For an example of how to do this, see the "Making the Grade" math project in the PBLWorks.org project library. Students learn about statistical analysis and measures of central tendency alongside learning theory about growth mindset as they develop informed recommendations for class- or school-level grading policies.)

- Promote individual accountability for contributing to a team effort. Have teams discuss how to handle situations when one or more members are not pulling their fair share of the load. (See information on team contracts in Chapter 4, "Managing Activities.") Consider asking teams to discuss, assess, and report on everyone's contribution, perhaps assigning points in proportion to effort.
- Finally, trust that over time as you build a culture for PBL, students will feel accountable to each other and help reinforce norms around fairness and effort.

Creating and Using Rubrics

As we said earlier, rubrics are an indispensable tool for assessment in a project. We'll offer some guidance specifically on their use in PBL. (For more on aligning rubrics with standards, see Chapter 2, "Aligning to Standards".)

A rubric is more than a tool to assess final products. It can be leveraged throughout the project to support formative assessment and promote reflection. Rubrics can be used to:

- *Make expectations transparent.* Students are more likely to succeed when they have a clear understanding of how their work will be assessed from the beginning of a project.
- *Cultivate a growth mindset.* Rubrics can help students track learning and improvement as they plan and revise their work. Ongoing use of rubrics and cycles of revision reinforce the idea that a first draft is a good start, but students should keep crafting, reflecting, and drafting until they make their final products public.
- *Give and receive feedback.* Meaningful feedback, guided by a clear formative evaluation tool and provided in the context of a structured protocol, improves the quality of student work and builds a culture of interdependence.

Here are some ideas for using rubrics throughout a project:

Project Phase	Rubric Uses & Tips
Project Launch: Provide time for students to analyze rubrics for each product they will create in the project. Do this before they ever start creating products.	Practice using the rubric on exemplars of work and the project's products to build understanding, if you have them from previous projects or can find similar work samples. Students are more likely to buy into the project expectations when they contribute to rubric creation. Consider co-constructing the rubric with students by dissecting an exemplar of the product for both content and style, and then identifying the indicators that all agree belong on the rubric.
Build Knowledge and Skills: Create a routine in which students use the rubric to reflect on what they know and what they need to know in order to move forward.	You may find it useful to set aside a specific day of the week to check status/progress with the rubric. Writing rubric checks into your project calendar is a helpful reminder for you and your students to take the time to assess and reflect.
Develop and Critique: Implement a regular routine in which students use the project rubric to self- and peer-assess progress.	Have students use the rubric in critique protocols. Use success skill rubrics for self- and peer-assessment of growth. The most effective revisions happen after taking time for reflection on the critique received. Make sure to build in these days up front when planning out how long your project will take.
Presentation: Have students use the rubric to self-reflect on their final products. Provide an annotated rubric to students along with their final project grade.	Reserve a good chunk of time the day after the culmination of a project for students to go over audience, teacher, and peer feedback to accurately assess their work one final time, before you do the final assessment.

Summative Assessment in PBL

Assessment *of* learning takes place near the end of a project. This is when you determine if the learning goals specified for the project were met. Summative assessment in PBL can take a variety of forms, depending on the project. You may need a combination of several pieces of evidence in order to get a more complete picture, such as:

- Scoring the final product against a rubric
- A performance task to find out whether students can apply what they have learned
- A test, essay, or other piece of writing that shows how well students understand concepts and have gained content knowledge
- Input from experts about students' final presentations or exhibitions of work

- Student journals, design notebooks, lab reports, or other written products that provide evidence of what students have learned

Your summative assessments and final reflections on the project might tell you that students did not meet learning goals. It's up to you to decide what to do about it: reteach something, if it's important, either in a future project or some other kind of lesson, or if it's not vital, just make a note and revise the project next time you do it.

PBL PRO TIP

Ask Outside Experts & Audiences to Help Assess

In addition to assessment by the teacher, themselves, and peers, students may be assessed by other people beyond the classroom. Experts who have been involved in the project can contribute to both formative and summative assessment. The same goes for end-users of a product or service, or stakeholders who will be impacted by the project.

The people with whom students share their final products can offer feedback to inform summative assessment. Here are some tips:

> Make sure the people giving feedback understand the project and expectations for products and presentations. Share a rubric or other set of criteria with them, to score students and record comments.

> Encourage presentation audience members to (gently) ask questions. Consider providing suggestions or question stems.

> In projects that are simulations, ask outside guests to play the role of stakeholders and explain how they should do so.

> If guests are experts in the topic, debrief with them after presentations to get their feedback on the project.

Some Final Thoughts

❯ Don't assess what you haven't taught—it's not fair to students. That basic advice applies to good teaching, not just PBL, but it's worth remembering. For example, if you're going to be assessing presentation skills, make sure you teach them during the project, if students haven't learned them before.

❯ Given the need for lots of formative assessment in PBL, it may sound like it's too much of a burden on the teacher—but remember, you're not alone! Involving students through self- and peer-assessment helps reduce the load. So does including other adults such as experts, mentors, and audiences in the assessment process.

❯ As we said in other places in this book, a major goal of PBL is to encourage students to be independent, self-directed learners. The same is true of assessment; think of being able to assess your own work, and to give and receive feedback, as essential success skills that will help students in their further education and on the job.

✳ NOTES ✳

CHAPTER 6

Scaffolding Student Learning

P ROVIDING SCAFFOLDS FOR STUDENTS—SUPPORTS
to help them learn new knowledge, concepts, or skills—is
a good example of something most teachers already know
how to do that can be reframed for a PBL context. Many of the
scaffolding strategies in your teaching toolbox can be used during
a project. But you may need some new tools, since PBL often does
call upon students to think and act in ways that are new to them, if
they've previously experienced mostly traditional instruction.

There's an important equity-related reason for scaffolding in PBL too. We want *all* students to reap the benefits PBL provides, regardless of their background, previous educational experiences, reading level, or language proficiency. Scaffolding allows students with diverse needs to gain access to a project and meet its goals for learning. However, it's important to understand a key aspect of scaffolding that makes it different from the more general term "support."

Scaffolding is support that gets students to a higher level, but is removed when no longer necessary. Think of scaffolding on the side of a building; once the building is constructed, the scaffolding is taken down. Or think of training wheels on a bike. It's the same with student learning. You want to encourage growth and independence, not "over-support" students. Zaretta Hammond (Hammond, 2020) explains it this way:

"Instructional equity happens when the teacher is scaffolding learning to the point that *the scaffold at some moment falls away, so that the student becomes independent.* Unfortunately, what I often see instead is over-scaffolding and permanent instructional crutches. Students remain dependent learners; they never internalize cognitive routines and procedures."

In this chapter you'll see many examples of how to support students during a project. As you use them, especially as you and they become more experienced with PBL, always keep this question in mind: Do my students still need this, or can they do it on their own?

Planning Scaffolding

A PBL teacher needs to plan scaffolding thoughtfully before launching a project *and* respond flexibly to student needs as the project progresses, informed by formative assessment. With practice and reflection, you'll get better at designing the specific supports that will best meet students' needs in PBL. As students encounter new challenges, they may need new types of scaffolds, but the goal is always the same: ever-expanding independence, confidence, and mastery.

"Scaffold Student Learning" in the Project Based Teaching Rubric:

❱ Each student receives necessary instructional supports to access content, skills, and resources; these supports are removed when no longer needed.

❱ Scaffolding is guided as much as possible by students' questions and needs; the teacher does not "front-load" too much information at the start of the project, but waits until it is needed or requested by students.

❱ Key success skills are taught using a variety of tools and strategies; students are provided with opportunities to practice and apply them, and reflect on progress.

❱ Student inquiry is facilitated and scaffolded, while allowing students to act and think as independently as possible.

Keep in mind, as you think about the scaffolding needed for a project, that scaffolds commonly used in many traditional classrooms can also be used in PBL, such as:

- Modeling with think-alouds
- Breaking a topic into parts
- Providing visual models
- Activating prior knowledge
- Connecting to student interests
- Using hands-on activities and manipulatives
- Providing analogies/metaphors
- Offering verbal cues and guiding questions

- Using graphic organizers/mind maps
- Showing examples
- Pre-teaching vocabulary
- Asking follow-up questions
- Using stories
- Creating opportunities for student conversation/discussion
- Providing context
- Offering sentence stems/language models

One of the keys to successful project implementation is identifying, during the planning phase, where students are likely to struggle and what scaffolds can be put in place to support them. An effective way to do this is to walk through your project through the eyes of your students.

Use what you know about your students—their strengths, areas of growth, interests, and struggles—and identify ahead of time what parts of the project they will be able to do and where they're more likely to need support. Use your previous experience to predict what kinds of needs exist in your classroom. Have you done projects that involve, say, the reading tasks before? Was everybody able to access the same material? Is it likely that these same needs will require scaffolding this time around? Be careful, though, not to blindly preload scaffolds based on previous projects. Students grow at different rates, so it's important that scaffolds are deployed only as needed.

A question to ask yourself when planning scaffolding is whether access to the scaffold might potentially benefit all students in your class. For example, if you want students to be engaging in academic conversations, you might teach a lesson early in the year in which you introduce sentence starters for these conversations, and then post a chart with the sentence starters on the classroom wall. Students who need the sentence starters can refer to them, while students who have internalized them can disregard.

However, it's also important to ask this question: Will reliance on this scaffold inhibit the growth, learning, or challenge of any students? You don't want to limit their opportunity for productive struggle. For example, some students may benefit from a structured outline template for a written assignment, while other students may benefit from the challenge of organizing their writing without this scaffold. You can determine which students would benefit from a given scaffold, and in other cases, you might help students self-determine the level of support and structure they might need.

Scaffolding Content and Process

Scaffolds can be quite versatile. Many of the same instructional strategies you use for scaffolding content can also be used when scaffolding the process for completing the project. Here are some examples:

Scaffolding Strategy	Example of Use to Scaffold Project Process	Example of Use to Scaffold Content
Modeling with think-alouds	Model how to generate student questions during a project launch	Model how to approach a challenging math scenario
Breaking a topic into parts	Analyze components of a collaboration rubric in small groups	Practice making hypotheses in science to support larger understanding of the scientific method
Using graphic organizers/ mind maps	Develop a timeline for the project	Complete a character analysis chart for reading fictional stories
Creating opportunities for student conversation/discussion	Teams pair up to critique one another's products/ presentations	Engage in a Socratic seminar on a controversial historical issue
Using routines and protocols	Use a gallery walk for students to give and receive feedback	Use the "Connect, Extend, Challenge" routine to help students make connections between prior knowledge and new ideas

Scaffolding Inquiry

"Sustained Inquiry" is one of the Essential Project Design Elements and it needs to be scaffolded, especially if students are relatively new to PBL. The process of asking their own questions, finding resources, and applying what they've learned to answer a driving question and create a product is complex. Students may think inquiry just means googling a topic—so you need to support them in building their independent thinking skills in a learner-centered classroom.

When planning scaffolding for inquiry, consider questions such as:

- What does inquiry look like in my subject area? How does the process work? What particular ways of thinking are required?
- Will basic brainstorming work for generating questions, or do I need to provide more structure to the process?
- Do I need to provide some foundational knowledge to inform students' first inquiry cycle?
- How can I give students opportunities to practice the various steps in the process, to prepare them for independent inquiry?

Scaffolding PBL for Students with Special Needs

Special education teacher Kristen Uliasz, who works at a high school in Davis, California, claims that "PBL has transformed my vision of inclusive special education for students with even the most significant support needs."

The engaging and dynamic learning environment PBL creates for all students is also known as the best way to serve students with a wide range of disabilities, Uliasz says. PBL provides these students with opportunities for real-world learning, building success skills, and peer relationships.

When planning scaffolding for special needs students, Uliasz offers three tips:

1. **Collaborate with colleagues.** When planning a project, regular education and special education teachers can team up to anticipate student needs and plan support. She notes that the "Universal Design for Learning" framework is helpful for seeing that scaffolds that are designed for certain students can actually benefit many students.

2. **Differentiate instruction.** PBL provides opportunities for differentiation when students make choices about how to work and what to create. There's also room in projects for conventional differentiation strategies like front-loading vocabulary, providing visual supports, or offering texts with varied reading levels.

3. **Embed IEP goals into projects.** Plan how to include a student's specific IEP goals throughout a project's pathway. A project provides frequent, authentic, natural opportunities to work on commonly seen goals such as communication, self-management, social skills, self-determination, and self-advocacy.

(drawn from the blog post "Inclusive Special Education via PBL" by Kristen Uliasz, 2016, at pblworks.org/blog)

Like we've said elsewhere in this book, we recommend regular use of a small set of tools and protocols that become familiar to students, such as those in the table below.

Tools and Protocols for Scaffolding Inquiry

Tool/Protocol	Description	What is it good for?
See, Think, Wonder (from Project Zero)	After looking at a set of images, documents, data points, etc., students describe what they see, what they think it means, and what questions it raises for them.	Beginning an inquiry process by making student thinking visible as they're introduced to new ideas.
Building Background Knowledge (from EL Education)	In this small group discussion protocol, students use chart paper with three concentric circles to discuss, in order, their prior knowledge about a topic, a shared text that they read together, and finally, an expert text unique to each student in the group.	Helping students connect to what they already know, and collaborate to make meaning of new, complex ideas.
Question Formulation Technique (QFT) (from The Right Question Institute)	A five step process to stimulate student thinking and develop a list of open-ended, high-level questions.	Making sure that students can ask good questions.
Graphic organizer or other note-taking document	A structure or frame for collecting information or recording students' findings in a specific format.	Organizing ideas and helping students learn how to prioritize information.
Resource guide	A handout or digital space with links, videos, websites, and articles vetted by the teacher. May include a list of search engines that are more likely to have resources available at their reading level, to help students avoid simply googling it.	Helping to narrow students' search area and stay focused on finding answers to their questions and discovering new ones.

Scaffolding Product Creation

To decide what supports students will need in order to create the final product for the project, break it down into incremental steps.

For example, a formal presentation using slides can be broken down into mini-lessons to scaffold understanding the content, the creation of the slides, the writing of the spoken part of the presentation, and fine-tuning it through practice. When broken apart, each of these steps provides assessment opportunities for both you and your students, and helps to make the task more manageable.

Similarly, showing exemplars or models of the final product will help students visualize their end goal. It will also help you identify areas where additional scaffolding might be needed and finalize the quality criteria you're looking for in a final product. Be careful, though, that students don't simply copy the exemplar—you don't want to narrow their thinking and choices. You could show an exemplar of a similar product that does not exactly fit the project, as long as the quality criteria for it are about the same.

Another great tool for scaffolding the product is a rubric that describes it. Sharing a rubric with students early and often will help them more clearly understand exactly what they're working toward.

PBL PRO TIP

Scaffold PBL for English Language Learners

As we said in the introduction, PBL works for all students, including those who are learning English, with the right support.

With scaffolding, you can reduce linguistic or cultural barriers to content or skill mastery and to project completion and success. You can also support students' acquisition of English language skills within the context of a project. To learn more and find examples of scaffolds, see the document in the appendix of this book, "English Learner Scaffolds for PBL."

You can also find a list of linked resources in a special blog post at *PBLWorks.org/blog/resources-list-english-learners-pbl.*

Scaffolding Success Skills

As important as it is to plan for and provide scaffolds for content, process, and products, you will also need to plan for and provide scaffolds for helping students develop the success skills you've identified for the project. We can't assume that students will naturally know how to think critically, problem-solve, collaborate, or communicate in the ways they need to in PBL.

Consider building success skills *before* launching a project, so students have a basic understanding of what these skills look and feel like when the project begins. Having students practice a success skill in a low-stakes situation, and where no new content is involved, helps them focus on the skill itself. Like protocols and routines, once a scaffold for a success skill becomes familiar to students, they can use it seamlessly when they need it, and save their cognitive energy for learning and other project tasks.

Scaffolds for success skills can be the same ones you'd use for scaffolding inquiry and process: rubrics, exemplars and modeling, routines and protocols, sentence starters, and so on. Here are some specific examples:

Critical thinking:
- Role-play different points of view on an issue, to help with perspective-taking.
- Use Socratic seminars, guided reading, concept mapping to help students understand difficult texts.
- Provide a set of questions to ask/things to check when evaluating the quality of a source of information.

Problem-solving:
- Model the steps for a problem-solving or troubleshooting process.

Collaboration:
- Model a decision-making process in fishbowl format.
- Provide a template for a team meeting agenda.

Communication:
- Provide a presentation planning form (see pblworks.org/resources for an example).
- Post sentence stems for "How to disagree politely."

Creativity:
- Teach steps in the process of innovation.
- Teach and use a design thinking process.
- Practice advanced brainstorming/idea-generation strategies (see resources at IDEO.com).

Project management:

- Provide a team work plan or team task log document (see pblworks.org/resources for an example).
- Teach a process for conflict resolution in teams (find an example and many more tools and resources from the Project Management Institute Educational Foundation at pmief.org).

Some Final Thoughts

Keep in mind that the purpose of scaffolding is not to prevent struggle. We do want our students to engage in challenging projects and processes, because it is in this zone of proximal development that students grow. We want to make sure students know we are there to support them, but not to remove all obstacles in their way.

Here are some reflective questions to remind you of what we've discussed in this chapter and provide further food for thought:

> Have I aligned my scaffolding with standards and other learning goals?

> How can I use formative assessment to help me understand what my students need in the project?

> Have I planned ways for students of various skill levels, including those with reading disabilities or language barriers, to access the information needed to successfully complete the project?

> How can I encourage students to become more self-directed learners who recognize their need for scaffolding and request it, rather than assume they need it?

CHAPTER 7

Engaging and Coaching Students

ONE OF THE MANY STRENGTHS OF PROJECT Based Learning is that, by design, it's an engaging way to teach and learn. Working on a project that is meaningful and relevant to their lives—and to the lives of others—draws students into the learning process and motivates them to engage in challenging work.

Much of the task of engaging students, then, includes what we covered in other chapters, especially Chapter 1, "Designing and Planning a Project." In this chapter, we'll explain more about how to keep students engaged throughout a project, starting with an "entry event" to ignite their interest and curiosity.

"Engage and Coach" in the Project Based Teaching Rubric:

❯ The teacher's knowledge of individual student strengths, interests, backgrounds, and lives is used to engage them in the project and inform instructional decision-making.

❯ Students and teacher use standards to co-define goals and benchmarks for the project (e.g., by co-constructing a rubric) in developmentally appropriate ways.

❯ Students' enthusiasm and sense of ownership of the project is maintained by the shared nature of the work between teachers and students.

❯ Student questions play the central role in driving the inquiry and product development process; the driving question is actively used to sustain inquiry.

❯ Appropriately high expectations for the performance of all students are clearly established, shared, and reinforced by teachers and students.

❯ Individual student needs are identified through close relationships built with the teacher; needs are met not only by the teacher but by students themselves or other students, acting independently.

❯ Students and the teacher reflect regularly and formally throughout the project on what (content) and how (process) students are learning; they specifically note and celebrate gains.

We'll also talk about the role of the "teacher as coach" in PBL. This aspect of Project Based Teaching is one of the more challenging for secondary teachers, because it's different from what they may see as their primary role in the traditional model of teaching, which is to transmit knowledge. It's been said that elementary school teachers "teach kids" whereas secondary teachers "teach subjects." That's not entirely true, of course, at either level, but for many teachers becoming a "coach" requires both a philosophical shift and a new skill set.

Engaging Students at the Project Launch: Entry Events

It's important to capture student interest and build excitement at the beginning of a project. It should feel like a special opportunity, not just another unit. The launch of a project typically features three components to engage students: the entry event, the driving question, and the generation of students' "need to know" questions.

Let's first look at entry events.

Sometimes a project is so naturally engaging that you don't need to generate student interest with a special event. Veteran PBL teachers know when this is the case. Oftentimes it's when a real-world problem or issue just *demands* a project. For example, when a social justice issue arises in the news, students may want to address it and a project can be co-created and begun right on the spot.

It could also be that you know your students well enough to trust that simply announcing a project and getting started on it will be enough to engage them. For example, if bullying is occurring in school and your students would jump at a chance to do something about it, a short discussion is all that's needed to get to work and begin the inquiry process. The same might be true of a project about something most teens would be primed to investigate, such as mobile phone plans, romantic relationships, or pop culture.

In each of these examples, it isn't an "event" per se that captures student interest and builds excitement; it arises naturally. For many projects, however, the teacher needs to plan an "entry event" that accomplishes this. After all, your students may not even know or have heard much about a topic that's important in the subject you teach. They may not be particularly interested in, say, Shakespeare, the Vietnam War, human evolution, or the misuse of statistics—it's up to you to engage them in a project in which they learn about those topics.

PBL PRO TIP

Tailor Entry Events Based on Knowledge of Students

When planning an entry event, ask yourself: How can I create an entry event experience for this project that speaks to this particular group of students—their interests, their passions, and their lived experiences?

For example, if the entry event involves a guest speaker or a presentation by an expert, try to find a speaker who comes from a similar background as the majority of your students. If you are selecting images, videos, statistics, or texts for students to explore in the entry event, be sure to leverage student interests as much as possible.

Even if you use the same project from year to year, you may want to modify or design a new entry event for each class so you can tailor it to that specific group of students.

An entry event is not simply a "hook," which teachers might be familiar with in traditional lesson planning. It's meant to get students to feel and think, not just get their attention. As high school math teacher and PBLWorks Emeritus National Faculty member Telannia Norfar says, her goal is to "grab students' hearts so their minds will follow." The event is also meant to provoke curiosity and generate questions to begin the inquiry process.

An entry event might require one class period, sometimes more, and can take many forms:

- Guest speaker
- Video clip from the internet, a film, or TV show
- Field trip or field work
- Piece of correspondence (real or simulated)
- Lively discussion

- Activity or simulation
- Song, poem, or art
- Startling set of statistics
- Provocative reading or website viewing
- Puzzling problem

Here are some examples of entry events in projects at pblworks.org:

The Scoop on Our Stuff:
Students examine a cotton t-shirt, and use a See, Think, Wonder protocol to engage in a discussion about where it really came from.

Revolutions Project:
Students participate in a simulation of an unjust society to learn about conditions that lead to revolutions.

Healthy School Challenge:
Students visit the school cafeteria, meet the person in charge, and participate in a school lunch taste test.

Crash Course!:
Students do an activity in teams, using materials provided to construct a device that will protect an egg when dropped.

Eco Writers:
Students receive a letter or video from a partner elementary school teacher who asks them to write a children's book for young students.

Engaging Students with the Driving Question

In Chapter 1, we talked about the purpose of the "driving question" in PBL and explained how to write one. Here, let's discuss how to introduce students to the driving question, or co-create it with them, in order to engage them in the project.

If you write a driving question when planning the project, roll it out to students with some fanfare. This typically happens right after the entry event. If they're already familiar with PBL, students will know how central the driving question is to a project. If they're new to PBL, explain the purpose and how they'll be using the driving question throughout the project.

Engage students in a discussion to be sure they understand the question and think it captures the project. Help students see how the driving question focuses their work. Also at this time, you might need to hand out or post a "project information sheet," or reveal the project wall (see Chapter 4), with an overview of the project and details about the major products.

Entry Events in Remote Learning

Teacher, PBL consultant and blogger Mike Kaechele posted these suggestions for entry events to use in remote learning:

❯ *Video with back channel discussion:* Make it a big event, prep students for it, and have the class watch it together, using the chat feature to react.

❯ *Guests on video conference:* Many people would be happy to talk with students online, since they don't need to take the time to travel to your classroom.

❯ *Virtual field trip:* Use virtual museums, webcams, or other virtual trips such as Google Expeditions.

❯ *Teacher field work:* Go on a trip yourself and record it, interviewing people, collecting data and information for the project.

❯ *Home field work:* Ask students to leave their screens and collect things, record images and sounds, or gather data.

❯ *Interviews:* Ask students to phone or video-conference with family, friends, or community members to get their views on an issue or topic.

❯ *Virtual simulations:* Run a virtual experiment or record yourself in a science lab. Use a popular game like Minecraft or Among Us as a launching point. Ask students to investigate scientific phenomenon or design their own (safe!) experiments at home with adult supervision.

Source: mikekaechele.com

If you did not write a driving question ahead of time, invite students to co-create one with you after the entry event, which increases their sense of agency and ownership in the project. This is generally more appropriate for students who are familiar with PBL.

Writing the driving question might be obvious. For example, in the situation mentioned earlier where bullying was occurring among students, the driving question could be as simple as, How can we reduce bullying at our school? which the class could agree on readily after a discussion of the problem.

For other projects, it may take more time to co-create the driving question. After the entry event, go over the criteria for a good driving question (see Chapter 1). Ask students to work in pairs or trios to write drafts of possible driving questions, then write a final draft as a whole class. Arrive at a whole-group consensus if at all possible— avoid the "majority vote" approach, which tends to disengage the minority.

Engaging Students in the Need to Know Process

Another important key to student engagement in PBL lies in the process of generating and using their own "need to know" questions. Giving students ownership over asking the questions central to the project is naturally motivating. They stay engaged through sustained inquiry as they continually seek answers and develop new questions throughout the project.

This process begins as part of the project launch, after students have been engaged by the entry event, know the driving question, and understand the basic information about the project. It typically takes about one class period. Here are the steps:

1. **Create a chart (on whiteboard, chart paper, or digitally) with three columns, to record the results of steps 2, 3 and 4:**

Know	Need to Know	Next Steps

2. **Invite students to think about what they already know about the topic and what skills they already have that will help them successfully complete the project.**
   This includes activating prior knowledge students can draw on. Prompt them to also consider things like community connections, people or experts who may be able to help with the project, technology tools they can use, and so on.

   Here are some tips:
   - Allow think time for students, first individually, then in pairs or small groups.
   - Don't spend too much time on the knows; move on to the need to knows. Students will have the opportunity to add new ideas to both lists over time.
   - Capture students' words just as they share them, in their voice, to create a sense of ownership.
   - Ask for clarification and permission to make minor edits when necessary.

3. **Invite students to think about what they need to know about the topic and what skills they will need to successfully complete the project.**
   Prompt students to consider content knowledge, concepts, and specific skills related to the driving question and the major products in the project.

   Tips, in addition to those above:
   - Give an example question or two if students are new to the process.
   - If you notice students are missing some important pieces of the puzzle, coach them to ask more questions.
   - You may have students record their questions on sticky notes so you can move them as they are answered.
   - At this step, don't worry if some of the students' questions are irrelevant. Figuring out what you actually need to know is part of the inquiry process.

4. **Invite students to think about what next steps they need to take.**
   Prompt students to consider how they would start the process of answering their questions. Encourage them to move beyond simple ideas like "We should do research." Probe for what specifically they would like to research, and how they would approach researching the question (e.g., by online search, asking experts, surveying users of a product, etc.).

5. **(Optional) Ask students to organize their questions into categories.**

    To further support students in getting to the heart of the project and asking the kinds of questions that will propel deep learning throughout, it can also be useful to have students organize their knows and need to knows into categories such as:

- Logistical/process/product-related (How long should the video be? Who are we presenting to?)
- Content-related (What's the history of immigration laws in the U.S.? What makes data reliable?)

PBL PRO TIP

Scaffold Question-Asking with the QFT

Students will need guidance and support in developing the ability to generate useful questions that will guide their inquiry throughout the project. One method for scaffolding this process is the "Question Formulation Technique" (QFT) created by the Right Question Institute.

After students brainstorm questions, they label them as either "close-ended" or "open-ended." Next, they practice changing open-ended questions to close-ended and vice versa. Students then identify their top three questions with a rationale for their prioritization. Finally, students share out their selected questions and reflect on the value of both types of questions. This helps students learn from one another and see the value of asking their own questions.

Revisiting the driving question and need to know list throughout a project

To keep students engaged in the inquiry process, revisit the driving question and their need to know questions frequently.

Establish a routine for regularly reflecting on the driving question to keep the focus on it and see how students' thinking about it may have evolved. Ask students if the question still captures the heart of the project or whether it needs revision.

Likewise, revisit the list of need to know questions. Move questions that have been answered to the "Know" column and add new questions to the "Need to Know" column. If you do this regularly, even at the beginning of each class meeting, it helps students review the previous day's learning and frames the upcoming learning experiences and work time as an opportunity for students to seek further answers to their questions. It can be very motivating for students to see their list of what they know growing day by day and to see how their new questions are becoming deeper and more sophisticated as well.

When revisiting the need to know questions with students, offer prompts such as:

- What questions have we answered?
- What new questions have emerged?
- What questions seem more or less important now?

Note: As they dig deeper, students may ask questions that are not directly relevant to completing the project but are nonetheless interesting and worth exploring. Invite students to investigate these questions on their own and allow time for sharing the results with the class.

Additional Tips for Keeping Students Engaged

Here are some questions to ask yourself during a project, if you sense that students are becoming disengaged:

1. **Am I providing the appropriate level of challenge and support?**
   In order to learn and grow, we need to be in the "stretch zone" (sometimes called the risk zone). If the challenge is too far out of reach, or we lack adequate support, we are in the frustration zone or danger zone and can disengage. If a task is too easy, we are in the "comfort zone" not developing any new knowledge or skills, which can also lead to disengagement.

So in addition to leveraging your knowledge of students' passions and interests in the design of the project, it's also important to apply your knowledge of their academic strengths and challenges to ensure that all students are set up for success in the project.

See more on providing support to students in Chapter 6, "Scaffolding Student Learning."

PBL PRO TIP

Prevent "Project Fatigue"

Teacher, author, and blogger John Spencer offers this advice
for keeping students engaged during projects:

❯ *Adjust your expectations.* If students appear to be burning out, give them more time to complete the project.

❯ *Use a design thinking framework.* Set clear phases in a project so students know they're going to be moving out of one (e.g., research) and into another (e.g., ideation).

❯ *Set benchmarks within your projects.* Establish short-term goals so students can feel like (and celebrate) they're making progress.

❯ *Take project breaks.* Pause project work for a day and do a team-builder, an activity to give team members a break from each other, or even a high-interest lesson on a different topic.

❯ *Be cognizant of multiple project demands.* If your school does a lot of PBL, students may feel overwhelmed with too many at once or no breaks in between them. Coordinate calendars among teachers so projects don't exactly overlap, and give students some "down time" between them by providing other kinds of learning experiences.

Source: "The Surprising Science of Project Fatigue (And How Teachers Can Help Prevent It)" blog post at spencerauthor.com

2. **Am I keeping things moving at the right pace?**

   One of the best ways to keep students engaged and motivated through the course of a project is to follow a schedule that is long enough to foster deep inquiry and learning and create quality products, but not so long that students become bored or fatigued. When you designed the project, you created a project calendar that we advised you to keep flexible. So if you notice that students are becoming disengaged, consider how you might shorten or speed up the project.

3. **Do I need to inject some new element into the project?**

   During a lengthy project, students' energy and engagement might drop off a bit in the "messy middle." A great way to re-ignite students' enthusiasm and increase their engagement is to help students see how the content and skills they are learning in the project are relevant in the "real world."

   Think in terms of the kinds of ideas that make entry events engaging. Consider inviting an expert to teach new content or give students feedback on their work in progress. Have students examine real-world/professional examples of the kinds of products they are working on. Engage the community members whose lives the project is designed to impact by having students survey or interview them. These kinds of experiences will help students gain new insights into what they're learning and also give them a boost of motivation to continue moving forward with the project.

   If your project is a simulation rather than a fully authentic, real-world project, you can boost engagement by introducing a pre-planned "twist" in the scenario or problem. For example, if your students are acting in the role of advisors to a fictitious company that wants them to help with marketing its products to teens, a memo could arrive that announces some constraints or a new development. (This kind of thing happens in real life, after all!)

Teacher as Coach

The teacher plays several roles in Project Based Learning; sometimes it's the traditional role of subject-matter expert, sometimes it's being a facilitator, and sometimes it's acting as a coach.

The metaphor "student-as-worker, teacher-as-coach" was popularized by education reformer Ted Sizer and it fits the PBL classroom well. He contrasted it with "the more familiar metaphor of "teacher as deliverer of instructional services" and advocated for "coaching students to learn how to learn and thus to teach themselves" (Sizer, 1990).

Teachers of music, art, and drama often play a coaching role, as do many career/ tech teachers when they coach students how to design something, fix a machine, or build a structure. Or think of what an athletic coach does:

- Communicates a vision of success
- Shares expertise about how to play the game or perform the action
- Organizes opportunities for application and practice
- Gives feedback on performance

- Pays attention to emotional well-being
- Cheers athletes on and celebrates successes

Teacher and PBL consultant Myla Lee (Lee, 2018) also compared "the best teachers" to her son's swim coach, offering these six coaching skills used by PBL teachers:

1. **Questioning**

   A coach asks probing questions intended to get students to think more deeply or differently, such as:

   - What makes you think that?
   - Why do you think this is the case?
   - What would have to change in order for …?
   - What would it look like if …?
   - What do you think would happen if…?"

2. **Listening**

   A coach actively listens to students, which includes:

   - Suspending judgment
   - Focusing intently on the student
   - Not interrupting, and providing pauses to allow the student time to think
   - Using body language to show they are "in tune," as evidenced by eye contact, leaning in to show interest, nodding in agreement, conveying empathy through facial expressions
   - Affirming what the student says by respectfully paraphrasing

3. **Formative assessment and feedback**

   A coach critiques student performance, pointing out what went well and where it fell short. According to Grant Wiggins, education reformer and co-founder of Understanding by Design (Wiggins, 2012), effective feedback has these seven characteristics:

   - goal-referenced
   - tangible and transparent
   - actionable
   - user-friendly (specific and personalized)
   - timely
   - ongoing
   - consistent

4. **Reflection**

   A coach helps students pause to think about feedback, what they need to know or do, and plan next steps. We made reflection one of the Essential Project Design Elements in our model for Gold Standard PBL because of its importance for cementing what is being learned in a project and for producing high-quality work. (See Chapter 4, "Managing Activities," for more on how to facilitate reflection throughout a project.)

5. **Gradual release of responsibility**

   A coach teaches with the goal of students being independently able to do something. Many teachers are already familiar with this idea, which has been called "I do, we do, you do" (Fisher & Frey, 2013) and "show them, help them, let them," which includes:

   - Modeling how to do a task
   - Supporting students with guided practice
   - Letting students do the task independently

6. **Affirmation and trust**

   A coach conveys faith in a student's ability, which helps build relational trust. As teacher, consultant, and author Rick Wormelli (Wormelli, 2016) points out, such trust is built from the first week of school. It comes from getting to know your students well, practicing empathy, and creating a collaborative culture of "we're in this together." (For more, see the section below on being a "warm demander" and Chapter 3, "Building the Culture.")

Adopting a "lead learner" stance

In order to position yourself as a coach in the classroom, it's valuable to take on the stance of a "lead learner," a concept often used in the context of being a school principal. Here, we use the term to mean working closely with and learning alongside your students during a project. Of course, you are still the subject-matter expert, and you designed the project, but if the driving question is truly open-ended then there is no "right answer" you know in advance. And since you should leave room for students to forge their own paths through the project, at least to some extent, they will surprise you and uncover new things you didn't anticipate, so you'll be learning *with* them.

Coaching in Remote Learning

When you're physically away from students, it can be harder to establish the rapport needed to be an effective coach. Here are some ideas for what you can do:

> Begin meetings with individuals or small groups with personal check-ins. Showing warmth and care is especially necessary online.

> Leverage videoconference breakout rooms or staggered schedules to facilitate small-group interactions and build relationships.

> Encourage students to communicate their feelings and needs with you in private, using email or other means.

> Use tech tools to conduct frequent "temperature checks" of the group and gauge students' affective and academic needs (e.g., polling tools, the text chat or reaction features of a video conferencing tool, or collaborative digital boards such as Padlet, Jamboard, or Nearpod Collaborate).

Here are some examples of what it looks like to be a lead learner:

- Make sure students see that you don't know the answer to the driving question and aren't trying to steer them down a certain path.
- Model genuine interest in the driving question or the problem being solved, and interest in the texts students read, websites and places they visit, videos they watch, and experts they hear from.
- "Think aloud" with students to show that you are truly wondering about aspects of the project and have your own questions.
- Think together about resources needed to help students complete the project. Be open to resources students find themselves, even though you may have planned to provide certain other resources.
- As we discussed in Chapter 1, "Designing and Planning a Project," you may even invite students to identify authentic problems, issues, and topics of interest to them to address in a project, then co-design it with them.

Being a "warm demander"

Another useful concept for acting as a coach in PBL is the "warm demander," which dates from the 1970s when Judith Cornfield described a teaching style that most benefitted native Alaskan students. It was further developed by Lisa Delpit (Delpit, 2013) who said warm demanders are teachers who "expect a great deal of their students, convince them of their own brilliance, and help them to reach their potential in a disciplined and structured environment."

Here's how Zaretta Hammond (Hammond, 2014) breaks down what a warm demander does—all of which apply to building the culture and being a coach in PBL:

- Explicit focus on building rapport and trust. Expresses warmth through non-verbal ways like smiling, touch, warm or firm tone of voice, and good-natured teasing.
- Shows personal regard for students by inquiring about important people and events in their lives.
- Earns the right to demand engagement and effort.
- Very competent with the technical side of instruction.
- Holds high standards and offers emotional support and instructional scaffolding to dependent learners for reaching the standards.
- Encourages productive struggle.
- Viewed by students as caring because of personal regard and "tough love" stance.

Coaching at the Completion of a Project

The last indicator in the "Engage & Coach" row of the Project Based Teaching Rubric emphasizes the role of reflection and states that students and the teacher "specifically note and celebrate gains" throughout a project. This is especially important when the project is coming to an end, because it helps students learn, and helps you learn—and it's deserved, after all the hard work.

After students have wrapped up their final products and made their work public, and any last summative assessment has been done, ask students to reflect on the knowledge, understanding, and skills they learned, how they learned and completed the project, and on the project design itself (which is helpful feedback for you). By now students are probably used to reflection routines, so use those once again (or try a new one, for this special purpose!) and ask students questions such as:

(About what they learned)

- Do you think you arrived at a satisfactory answer to the driving question?
- What more might you want to learn about this topic?
- What was the most valuable thing you learned?
- What success skills did you gain or improve upon?
- Did you meet your goals in this project? What new goals do you want to set for the next one?

(About how they learned)

- What parts of the project were most challenging? Why? What parts went smoothly?
- What were some problems or obstacles you had to overcome? How did you do it?
- How well did your team work together? How could you improve your collaboration skills next time?

(About the project)

- What worked well, and what could be improved about the project?
- What specific resources or lessons were most helpful? What more might be needed if this project is done again?
- Do you think you made a difference? Did you meet a need?

Finally, ask students to celebrate how much they have done in the project. Tell them what you think is especially worth celebrating. And consider these five ideas to more publicly or formally celebrate a project:

1. Invite audience members to stay around after presentations for a reception, to talk informally with students and offer praise.
2. Invite school and/or district administrators who were aware of the project, or outside experts, community members, and parents who were involved, to visit your classroom and offer congratulations.
3. In a whole-class activity, create a list of "What We Are Proud Of" or "Our Shining Moments."
4. Let your community know. Get a local reporter for a newspaper or radio or TV station to cover your project and tout the results. Arrange for project work to be displayed at a local government office, business, public library, museum, gallery, community center, etc.

5. Create an archive or "memorial" of some kind. Students could create a display of their work, contribute words or phrases to a signed "This Project Was…" poster to go on the classroom wall, assemble images and writing in a scrapbook, or place project artifacts in an online archive. These memorials could be kept with pride all year, shown to parents, visitors, administrators and colleagues, and to other students as helpful examples of what good PBL looks like.

Some Final Thoughts

Some common themes in this chapter overlap with what we've said in other chapters: Engaging and coaching students in PBL requires that you know your students well, and that you continually look for ways to help them connect with and make meaning from the learning experience. It requires you to recognize and build on their strengths, find ways to bring out their capabilities, and leverage opportunities to help them grow.

We'll end this chapter with a related message from Linda Darling-Hammond at the Learning Policy Institute. In a presentation for the California Department of Education in January 2021, she shared two principles from the science of learning and development that connect directly to being a coach in PBL:

> Relationships are the essential ingredient that catalyzes healthy development and learning.

> Students' perceptions of their own ability influence learning.

In Closing...

We wish you well on your PBL journey, whether you're just starting out, well underway, or have taken the trail many times already. You're doing important work! Today's students need engaging, meaningful learning—and our world needs them to be active citizens and problem solvers. Students who are furthest from educational opportunity especially benefit from PBL and Project Based Teaching, so we hope to see more of it in the schools that serve them.

It's taken a long time for Project Based Learning to become more widely used in education. It still has a long way to go, despite increased attention in recent years from teachers, school leaders, education policymakers, curriculum providers, and the media. It's certainly not yet the predominant pedagogy in the vast majority of K–12 schools.

There are many reasons for this, chief among them the long-held beliefs about what and how students should be taught—and how learning is measured—that have been with us for well over a century. We trust that, when done well according to the guidance in this book, the projects done by teachers and students will provide even more convincing evidence of the need for change. As a PBL teacher or leader, you're part of a profound effort to shift education in new directions.

You can find lots of resources for continued professional learning on our website, PBLWorks.org. And stay in touch: connect with @PBLWorks on social media, and share your PBL questions and stories with us. We're here for you!

✱ NOTES ✱

APPENDIX

*These materials are occasionally updated;
check PBLWorks.org/resources for the latest versions.*

Project Design Rubric

	Lacks Features of Effective PBL	Needs Further Development	Includes Features of Effective PBL
	The project has one or more of the following problems in each area:	*The project includes some features of effective PBL but has some weaknesses:*	*The project has the following strengths:*
Student Learning Goals: Key Knowledge Understanding & Success Skills	• Student learning goals are not clear and specific; the project is not focused on standards. • The project does not explicitly target, assess, or scaffold the development of success skills.	• The project is focused on standards-derived knowledge and understanding, but it may target too few, too many, or less important goals. • Success skills are targeted, but there may be too many to be adequately taught and assessed.	• The project is focused on teaching students specific and important knowledge, understanding, and skills derived from standards and central to academic subject areas. • Success skills are explicitly targeted to be taught and assessed, such as critical thinking, collaboration, creativity, and project management.

Essential Project Design Elements: Challenging Problem or Question	• The project is not focused on a central problem or question (it may be more like a unit with several tasks); or the problem or question is too easily solved or answered to justify a project.
	• The central problem or question is not framed by a driving question for the project, or it is seriously flawed, for example:
	  – it has a single or simple answer.
	  – it is not engaging to students (it sounds too complex or "academic" like it came from a textbook or appeals only to a teacher).
		• The project is focused on a central problem or question, but the level of challenge might be inappropriate for the intended students.
		• The driving question relates to the project but does not capture its central problem or question (it may be more like a theme).
		• The driving question meets some of the criteria (in the Includes Features column) for an effective driving question, but lacks others.
			• The project is focused on a central problem or question, at the appropriate level of challenge.
			• The project is framed by a driving question, which is:
			  – open-ended; there is more than one possible answer.
			  – understandable and inspiring to students.
			  – aligned with learning goals; to answer it, students will need to gain the intended knowledge, understanding, and skills.

Sustained Inquiry	• The "project" is more like an activity or "hands-on" task, rather than an extended process of inquiry. • There is no process for students to generate questions to guide inquiry.	• Inquiry is limited (it may be brief and only occur once or twice in the project; information-gathering is the main task; deeper questions are not asked). • Students generate questions, but while some might be addressed, they are not used to guide inquiry and do not affect the path of the project.	• Inquiry is sustained over time and academically rigorous (students pose questions, gather & interpret data, develop and evaluate solutions or build evidence for answers, and ask further questions). • Inquiry is driven by student-generated questions throughout the project.
Authenticity	• The project resembles traditional "schoolwork;" it lacks a real-world context, tasks and tools, does not make a real impact on the world or speak to students' personal interests.	• The project has some authentic features, but they may be limited or feel contrived.	• The project has an authentic context, involves real-world tasks, tools, and quality standards, makes an impact on the world, and/or speaks to students' personal concerns, interests, or identities.
Student Voice & Choice	• Students are not given opportunities to express their voice and make choices affecting the content or process of the project; it is teacher-directed. • (Or) Students are expected to work too much on their own, without adequate guidance from the teacher and/or before they are capable.	• Students are given limited opportunities to express their voice and make choices, generally in less important matters (deciding how to divide tasks within a team or which website to use for research). • Students work independently from the teacher to some extent, but they could do more on their own.	• Students have opportunities to express their voice and make choices on important matters (topics to investigate, questions asked, texts and resources used, people to work with, products to be created, use of time, organization of tasks). • Students have opportunities to take significant responsibility and work as independently from the teacher as is appropriate, with guidance.
Reflection	• Students and the teacher do not engage in reflection about what and how students learn or about the project's design and management.	• Students and teachers engage in some reflection during the project and after its culmination, but not regularly or in depth.	• Students and teachers engage in thoughtful, comprehensive reflection both during the project and after its culmination, about what and how students learn and the project's design and management.

	Lacks Features of Effective PBL	Needs Further Development	Includes Features of Effective PBL
	The project has one or more of the following problems in each area:	The project includes some features of effective PBL but has some weaknesses:	The project has the following strengths:
Critique & Revision	• Students get only limited or irregular feedback about their products and work-in-progress, and only from teachers, not peers. • Students do not know how or are not required to use feedback to revise and improve their work.	• Students are provided with opportunities to give and receive feedback about the quality of products and work-in-progress, but they may be unstructured or only occur once. • Students look at or listen to feedback about the quality of their work, but do not substantially revise and improve it.	• Students are provided with regular, structured opportunities to give and receive feedback about the quality of their products and work-in-progress from peers, teachers, and if appropriate from others beyond the classroom. • Students use feedback about their work to revise and improve it.
Public Product	• Students do not make their work public by presenting it to an audience or offering it to people beyond the classroom.	• Student work is made public only to classmates and the teacher. • Students present products, but are not asked to explain how they worked and what they learned.	• Student work is made public by presenting, displaying, or offering it to people beyond the classroom. • Students are asked to explain the reasoning behind choices they made, their inquiry process, how they worked, what they learned, etc.

Project Based Teaching Rubric

Project Based Teaching Practice	Beginning PBL Teacher	Developing PBL Teacher	Gold Standard PBL Teacher
Design & Plan	• Project includes some Essential Project Design Elements, but not at the highest level of the Project Design Rubric. • Plans for scaffolding and assessing student learning lack some detail; project calendar needs more detail, or is not followed. • Some resources for the project have not been anticipated or arranged in advance.	• Project includes all Essential Project Design Elements, but some are not at the highest level of the Project Design Rubric. • Plans for scaffolding and assessing student learning lack some details; project calendar allows too much or too little time, or is followed too rigidly to respond to student needs. • Most resources for the project have been anticipated and arranged in advance.	• Project includes all Essential Project Design Elements as described on the Project Design Rubric. • Plans are detailed and include scaffolding and assessing student learning and a project calendar, which remains flexible to meet student needs. • Resources for the project have been anticipated to the fullest extent possible and arranged well in advance.
Align to Standards	• Criteria for products are given but are not specifically derived from standards. • Scaffolding of student learning, critique and revision protocols, assessments and rubrics do not refer to or support student achievement of specific standards.	• Criteria for some products are not specified clearly enough to provide evidence that students have met all targeted standards. • Scaffolding of student learning, critique and revision protocols, assessments and rubrics do not always refer to or support student achievement of specific standards.	• Criteria for products are clearly and specifically derived from standards and allows demonstration of mastery. • Scaffolding of student learning, critique and revision protocols, assessments and rubrics consistently refer to and support student achievement of specific standards.
Build the Culture	• Norms are created to guide project work, but they may still feel like "rules" imposed and monitored by the teacher. • Students are asked for their ideas and given some choices to make, but opportunities for student voice and choice are infrequent or are only related to minor matters. • Students occasionally work independently, but often look to the teacher for guidance.	• Norms to guide the classroom are co-crafted with students, and students are beginning to internalize these norms. • Student voice and choice is encouraged through intentionally designed opportunities, e.g., when choosing teams, finding resources, using critique protocols, or creating products. • Students work independently to some extent, but look to the teacher for direction more often than necessary.	• Norms to guide the classroom are co-crafted with and self-monitored by students. • Student voice and choice is regularly leveraged and ongoing, including identification of real-world issues and problems students want to address in projects. • Students usually know what they need to do with minimal direction from the teacher.

Project Based Teaching Practice	Beginning PBL Teacher	Developing PBL Teacher	Gold Standard PBL Teacher
Build the Culture *continued*	• Student teams are often unproductive or require frequent intervention by the teacher. • Students feel like there is a "right answer" they are supposed to give, rather than asking their own questions and arriving at their own answers; they are fearful of making mistakes. • Value is placed on "getting it done" and time is not allowed for revision of work; "coverage" is emphasized over quality and depth.	• Student teams are generally productive and are learning what it means to move from cooperation to effective collaboration; the teacher occasionally has to intervene or manage their work. • Students understand there is more than one way to answer a driving question and complete the project, but are still cautious about proposing and testing ideas in case they are perceived to be "wrong." • The values of critique and revision, persistence, rigorous thinking, and pride in doing high-quality work are promoted by the teacher but not yet owned by students.	• Students work collaboratively in healthy, high-functioning teams, much like an authentic work environment; the teacher rarely needs to be involved in managing teams. • Students understand there is no single "right answer" or preferred way to do the project, and that it is OK to take risks, make mistakes, and learn from them. • The values of critique and revision, persistence, rigorous thinking, and pride in doing high-quality work are shared, and students hold each other accountable to them.
Manage Activities	• The classroom features some individual and team work time and small group instruction, but too much time is given to whole group instruction. • Classroom routines and norms for project work time are not clearly established; time is not used productively. • Schedules, checkpoints, and deadlines are set, but they are loosely followed or unrealistic; bottlenecks impede workflow. • Teams are formed using either a random process (e.g., counting off) or students are allowed to form their own teams with no formal criteria or process.	• The classroom features individual and team work time, whole group and small group instruction, but these structures are not well-balanced throughout the project. • Classroom routines and norms are established for project work time, but are not consistently followed; productivity is variable. • Realistic schedules, checkpoints, and deadlines are set, but more flexibility is needed; bottlenecks sometimes occur. • Generally well-balanced teams are formed, but without considering the specific nature of the project; students have too much voice and choice in the process, or not enough.	• The classroom features an appropriate mixture of individual and team work time, whole group and small group instruction. • Classroom routines and norms are consistently followed during project work time to maximize productivity. • Project management tools (group calendar, contract, learning log, etc.) are used to support student self-management and independence. • Realistic schedules, checkpoints, and deadlines are set but flexible; no bottlenecks impede workflow. • Well-balanced teams are formed according to the nature of the project and student needs, with appropriate student voice and choice.

Scaffold Student Learning	• Students receive some instructional supports to access both content and resources, but many individual needs are not met. • Teacher may "front-load" content knowledge before the project launch, instead of waiting for "need to know" points during the project. • Students gain key success skills as a side effect of the project, but they are not taught intentionally. • Students are asked to do research or gather data, but without adequate guidance; deeper questions are not generated based on information gathered.	• Most students receive instructional supports to access both content and resources, but some individual needs are not met. • Scaffolding is guided to some extent by students' questions and "need to knows" but some of it may still be "front-loaded." • Key success skills are taught, but students need more opportunities to practice success skills before applying them. • Student inquiry is facilitated and scaffolded, but more is needed; or, teacher may over-direct the process and limit independent thinking by students.	• Each student receives necessary instructional supports to access content, skills, and resources; these supports are removed when no longer needed. • Scaffolding is guided as much as possible by students' questions and needs; teacher does not "front-load" too much information at the start of the project, but waits until it is needed or requested by students. • Key success skills are taught using a variety of tools and strategies; students are provided with opportunities to practice and apply them, and reflect on progress. • Student inquiry is facilitated and scaffolded, while allowing students to act and think as independently as possible.
Assess Student Learning	• Student learning of subject-area standards is assessed mainly through traditional means, such as a test, rather than products; success skills are not assessed. • Team-created products are used to assess student learning, making it difficult to assess whether individual students have met standards. • Formative assessment is used occasionally, but not regularly or with a variety of tools and processes. • Protocols for critique and revision are not used, or they are informal; feedback is superficial, or not used to improve work.	• Project products and other sources of evidence are used to assess subject-area standards; success skills are assessed to some extent. • Individual student learning is assessed to some extent, not just team-created products, but teacher lacks adequate evidence of individual student mastery. • Formative assessment is used on several occasions, using a few different tools and processes. • Structured protocols for critique and revision and other formative assessments are used occasionally; students are learning how to give and use feedback.	• Project products and other sources of evidence are used to thoroughly assess subject-area standards as well as success skills. • Individual student learning is adequately assessed, not just team-created products. • Formative assessment is used regularly and frequently, with a variety of tools and processes. • Structured protocols for critique and revision are used regularly at checkpoints; students give and receive effective feedback to inform instructional decisions and students' actions.

Project Based Teaching Practice	Beginning PBL Teacher	Developing PBL Teacher	Gold Standard PBL Teacher
Assess Student Learning *continued*	• Students assess their own work informally, but the teacher does not provide regular, structured opportunities to do so. • Rubrics are used to assess final products, but not as a formative tool; or, rubrics are not derived from standards.	• Opportunities are provided for students to self-assess their progress, but they are too unstructured or infrequent. • Standards-aligned rubrics are used by the teacher to guide both formative and summative assessment.	• Regular, structured opportunities are provided for students to self-assess their progress and, when appropriate, assess peers on their performance. • Standards-aligned rubrics are used by students and the teacher throughout the project to guide both formative and summative assessment.
Engage & Coach	• The teacher has some knowledge of students' strengths, interests, backgrounds, and lives, but it does not significantly affect instructional decision-making. • Project goals are developed without seeking student input. • Students are willing to do the project as if it were another assignment, but the teacher does not create a sense of ownership or fuel motivation. • The driving question is presented at the project launch and student questions are generated, but they are not used to guide inquiry or product development. • Expectations for the performance of all students are not clear, too low, or too high.	• The teacher has general knowledge of students' strengths, interests, backgrounds, and lives and considers it when teaching the project. • Project goals and benchmarks are set with some input from students. • Students are excited by the project and motivated to work hard by the teacher's enthusiasm and commitment to their success. • Students' questions guide inquiry to some extent, but some are answered too quickly by the teacher; students occasionally reflect on the driving question. • Appropriately high expectations for the performance of all students are set and communicated by the teacher.	• The teacher's knowledge of individual student strengths, interests, backgrounds, and lives is used to engage them in the project and inform instructional decision-making. • Students and the teacher use standards to co-define goals and benchmarks for the project (e.g., by co-constructing a rubric) in developmentally appropriate ways. • Students' enthusiasm and sense of ownership of the project is maintained by the shared nature of the work between teachers and students. • Student questions play the central role in driving the inquiry and product development process; the driving question is actively used to sustain inquiry.

Engage & Coach
continued

• There is limited relationship-building in the classroom, resulting in student needs that are not identified or addressed. • Students and the teacher informally reflect on what and how students are learning (content and process); reflection occurs mainly at the end of the project.	• Student needs for further instruction or practice, additional resources, redirection, troubleshooting, praise, encouragement, and celebration are identified through relationship-building and close observation and interaction. • Students and the teacher occasionally reflect on what and how students are learning (content and process).	• Appropriately high expectations for the performance of all students are clearly established, shared, and reinforced by teachers and students. • Individual student needs are identified through close relationships built with the teacher; needs are met not only by the teacher but by students themselves or other students, acting independently. • Students and the teacher reflect regularly and formally throughout the project on what and how students are learning (content and process); they specifically note and celebrate gains and accomplishments.

Project Planner

1. Project Overview

Project Title	
Driving Question	
Grade Level/Subject	
Time Frame	
Public Product(s) (Individual and Team)	
Project Summary	

2. Learning Goals

Standards	
Literacy Skills	
Success Skills	
Key Vocabulary	
Rubric(s)	

3. Project Milestones

Directions: Use this section to create a high-level overview of your project. Think of this as the broad outline of the story of your project, with the milestones representing the significant 'moments' or 'stages' within the story. As you develop these, consider how the inquiry process is unfolding and what learning will take place. The Project Calendar (Section 4) will allow you to build out the milestones in greater detail.

Milestone #1 Entry Event	Milestone #2	Milestone #3	Milestone #4	Milestone #5	Milestone #6 Public Product
Key Student Question	Key Student Question	Key Student Question	Key Student Question	Key Student Question	Key Student Question
Formative Assessment(s)	Formative Assessment(s)	Formative Assessment(s)	Formative Assessment(s)	Formative Assessment(s)	Summative Assessment(s)

4. Project Calendar

Driving Question:					
Week:	Project Milestone:				
Key Student Question(s):					
Day 1:	Day 2:	Day 3:	Day 4:	Day 5:	
Notes:					

Driving Question:					
Week:	Project Milestone:				
Key Student Question(s):					
Day 1:	Day 2:	Day 3:	Day 4:	Day 5:	
Notes:					

English Learner Scaffolds for PBL

The chart below provides scaffolding strategies and recommendations to support English Learners during each phase of the project process. The recommendations here align with the planned scaffolding strategies from the *Theoretical Foundations and Research Base for California's English Language Development Standards*, provided at the end of this document

	Scaffolding the Project Process *How can you reduce linguistic or cultural barriers to project completion and success?*	Scaffolding Content Learning *How can you reduce linguistic or cultural barriers to content or skill mastery?*	Scaffolding Language Development *How can you support students' acquisition of English language skills within the context of a project?*
Launching the Project: Entry Event + Driving Question	• Have students develop and use a BIE Project Team Work Plan to structure and organize their project work. [2,5] • Post due dates and tasks to be completed to a project wall (virtual or in the classroom). [2] • Use the Question Formulation Technique to help students understand how to create effective questions. [6] • Provide closed and open sentence frames to support question generation. • Brainstorm and sort the questions generated by students. Sort questions into categories that are easy for students to identify (e.g., Content Questions, Process Questions, Presentation Questions). [8]	• Use a KWL chart[7], question frames, and explicit modeling[8] for the need to know list to help capture what students already know about the topic and to support students in asking new questions. [1,6] • During an entry event, use visual aids (e.g., photos, videos, physical objects) to help build context for learners at all levels of language proficiency.[7] • If the entry event is an "experience" (e.g., field trip, hands — on activity), have students use graphic organizers to keep their thoughts organized, or to write key words that can serve as memory triggers. A scavenger hunt is an useful strategy for a field trip.[7] • Use a camera, if possible, for students to capture experiences during the entry event or allow students to create visuals that they can later use to recall information and develop connections.[7]	• Explicitly teach and define content-related vocabulary during the discussion of the entry event.[2] • Create and maintain a vocabulary wall for academic language associated with the project.[8] • Use entry events as an opportunity to introduce students to different types of texts, and to discuss the conventions and purposes of text types.[4,8] • To provide more opportunities for low-stakes speaking and listening practice, have students discuss the entry event and need to knows in pairs or small groups before engaging in a whole-class discussion.[5] • Avoid (or explicitly teach) colloquialisms and idioms in project-related resources (e.g., entry events, driving questions, rubrics).[4]
Build Knowledge, Understanding and Skills to Answer Driving Question	• Post daily objectives, in student friendly language ("I Can....") for content, skills, and language learning.	• Deliver instruction in a variety of formats (e.g., hands-on learning experiences, small group lessons, direct instruction, etc.)[7]	• Use observations and written tasks such as reflective journals to formatively assess student progress on language development targets.[3]

	Scaffolding the Project Process *How can you reduce linguistic or cultural barriers to project completion and success?*	Scaffolding Content Learning *How can you reduce linguistic or cultural barriers to content or skill mastery?*	Scaffolding Language Development *How can you support students' acquisition of English language skills within the context of a project?*
Build Knowledge, Understanding and Skills to Answer Driving Question *continued*	• Refer to these often. Note when objectives are differentiated for specific students.[2] • Use a variety of grouping strategies (heterogeneous, language level, pairs, self-selected, etc.) strategically throughout the course of a project.[5]	• Provide leveled texts for students during work time.[4] • Structure workshops in a logical sequence, providing clear modeling and explanation as well as opportunities for guided practice.[2] • Have students work in linguistically diverse pairs or small groups to engage in reciprocal teaching of project content.[5] • Plan frequent opportunities for informal formative assessments (e.g., exit tickets, journals, whip-arounds, conferences), and adjust instruction based on these assessments.[3]	• Have students develop personalized illustrated dictionaries to keep track of key vocabulary.[8] • Provide varied opportunities for speaking and listening (e.g, inner-outer circles, think-pair-share, Jigsaw, role-plays).[5]
Develop and Critique Products and Answers to the Driving Question	• Model and practice the use of structured protocols for critiquing work.[8] • Provide Thinking Maps to help students organize ideas and information.[7] • Co-create rubrics for final products and success skills with students. Both teachers and students should use the rubrics for assessment and reflection, and the same rubrics should be used for formative and summative assessment.[3]	• Use the Question Formulation Technique to guide students in developing new questions to refine their understanding of content.[6]	• Provide sentence frames to help students give and receive feedback.[8] • When appropriate, provide students with exemplary writing samples and/or text frames to teach them about text and language conventions.[8]

Present Products and Answers to the Driving Question	• Have students work in groups to complete a BIE Presentation Plan[7] • Provide multiple opportunities for students to practice their presentations and receive feedback.[2,3] • Record students as they practice presentations. Allow them to review the video and compare their performance to the presentation rubric, reflecting on opportunities for improvements.[3]	• Provide graphic organizers to help students organize their learning when observing one another's presentations.[7] • Encourage students to use visual aids and multimedia to enhance and clarify the content in their presentations.[7] • Have students use structured protocols to reflect on how this project built on their existing knowledge and skills.[1]	• Work with students to identify the tone, level of formality, and linguistic style that are most appropriate for the presentation audience and context. Provide models to help students understand the appropriate "register."[8] • Provide language models for different aspects of presentations (e.g., giving instructions, describing processes, comparing and contrasting ideas.)[8] • Provide question frames to support audience members in asking effective questions.[6]

Planned Scaffolding Strategies from California Department of Education. (2012). Appendix C: Theoretical Foundations and Research Base for California's English Language Development Standards. Retrieved from a:
http://www.cde.ca.gov/sp/el/er/documents/eldstndspublication14.pdf

1. Taking into account what students already know, including primary language and culture, and relating it to what they are to learn.
2. Selecting and sequencing tasks, such as modeling and explaining, and providing guided practice, in a logical order.
3. Frequently checking for understanding during instruction, as well as gauging progress at appropriate intervals throughout the year.
4. Choosing texts carefully for specific purposes (e.g., motivational, linguistic, content).
5. Providing a variety of collaborative grouping processes.
6. Constructing good questions that promote critical thinking and extended discourse.
7. Using a range of information systems, such as graphic organizers, diagrams, photographs, videos, or other multimedia to enhance access to content.
8. Providing students with language models, such as sentence frames/starters, academic vocabulary walls, language frame charts, exemplary writing samples, or teacher language modeling (e.g., using academic vocabulary or phrasing).

REFERENCES

Adams, L. (2020). "PBL + SEL + Trauma-Informed Teaching for the Times We're In" blog post, PBLWorks.

Blumenfeld, P. C., Solloway, E., Marx, R. W., Krajcik, J. S., Guzdial, M., & Palincsar, A. (1991). "Motivating Project Based Learning: Sustaining the Doing, Supporting the Learning." *Educational Psychologist, 26*(3&4), 369–398.

Brophy, J. E. (2013). *Motivating Students to Learn.* New York, NY: Routledge.

Capon, N., & Kuhn, D. (2004). "What's So Good About Problem-Based Learning?" *Cognition and Instruction, 22*(1), 61–79.

Cheyne, M. (2014). "Optimizing Student Learning with Complex Instruction" blog post, Knowles Teacher Initiative.

Cohen, E., & Lotan, R. (2014). *Designing Groupwork: Strategies for the Heterogeneous Classroom.* New York, NY: Teachers College Press.

Costa, A., & Kallick, B. (2008). *Learning and Leading with Habits of Mind.* Alexandria, VA: ASCD.

Delpit, L. (2013). *Multiplication is for White People: Raising Expectations for Other People's Children.* New York, NY: The New Press.

Dochy, F., Segers, M., Van den Bossche, P., & Gijbels, D. (2003). "Effects of Problem-Based Learning: A Meta-Analysis." *Learning and Instruction, 13*(5), 533–568.

Duke, N., Halvorsen, A-L., Strachan, S. L., Kim, J., Konstantopoulos, S. (2020). "Putting PBL to the Test: The Impact of Project-based Learning on Second-grade Students' Social Studies and Literacy Learning and Motivation," 1-41. *American Educational Research Journal.*

Fisher, D., & Frey, N. (2013). *Better Learning Through Structured Teaching: A Framework for the Gradual Release of Responsibility, 2nd Edition.* Alexandria, VA: ASCD.

Haberman, M. (1991). "The Pedagogy of Poverty Versus Good Teaching." *Phi Delta Kappan.*

Hammond, Z. (2020). "A Conversation About Instructional Equity with Zaretta Hammond" blog post, Collaborative Classroom.

Hammond, Z. (2014). *Culturally Responsive Teaching and the Brain.* Thousand Oaks, CA: Corwin.

Hung, W., Jonassen, D. H., & Liu, R. (2007). "Problem-Based Learning." In J. M. Spector, J. G. van Merriënboer, M. D. Merrill, & M. Driscoll (Eds.), *Handbook of Research on Educational Communications and Technology* (3rd ed., pp. 1503–1581). Mahwah, NJ: Erlbaum.

Kingston, S. (2018). "Project Based Learning and Student Achievement." PBLWorks.

Krajcik, J. (2021). "Project-Based Learning Increases Science Achievement in Elementary School and Advances Social and Emotional Learning." Lucas Education Research.

Ladson-Billings, G. (1994). *The Dreamkeepers. Successful Teachers of African American Children.* San Francisco, CA: Jossey-Bass Publishing Co.

Larmer, J. (2013). "Project Based Learning vs. Problem Based Learning vs. XBL" blog post, PBLWorks.

Lee, M. (2018). "Coaching Your Students: Team PBL!" blog post, PBLWorks.

Maitra, D. (2017). "Funds of Knowledge: An Underrated Tool for School Literacy and Student Engagement." *International Journal of Society, Culture & Language.*

McTighe, J. (2017). "Beware of the Test Prep Trap" blog post, PBLWorks.

Mergendoller, J. (2017). "Defining High Quality PBL: A Look at the Research." HQPBL.org.

Rey, L. (2017). "How My Project-Based School Prepared Me for Columbia" blog post, PBLWorks.

Saavedra, A.R., Rapaport, A., & Morgan, K. (2021). "Knowledge in Action Efficacy Study Over Two Years." USC Dornsife Center for Economic and Social Research.

Sizer, T. (1990). "Common Principles." Coalition of Essential Schools.

Strobel, J., & van Barneveld, A. (2009). "When is PBL More Effective? A Meta-synthesis of Meta-analyses Comparing PBL to Conventional Classrooms." *Interdisciplinary Journal of Problem-based Learning, 3*(1).

Wells, J. (2020). "From Poster to Practice: How to Fulfill the Promise of Graduate Profiles" blog post, PBLWorks.

Wiggins, G. (2012). "Seven Keys to Effective Feedback." *Educational Leadership*, ASCD.

Wiggins, G., & McTighe, J. (2012). "Introduction: What is the UbD Framework?" ASCD.

Wormelli, R. (2016). "What to Do in Week One?" *Educational Leadership*, ASCD.

INDEX

* NOTES *